FINDING
HAPPINESS
IN THE MOST
UNLIKELY
PLACES

Donald W.
McCullough

With Study Questions
for Individuals or Groups

INTERVARSITY PRESS
DOWNERS GROVE, ILLINOIS 60515

InterVarsity Press is the book-publishing division of InterVarsity Christian Fellowship, a student movement active on campus at hundreds of universities, colleges and schools of nursing in the United States of America, and a member movement of the International Fellowship of Evangelical Students. For information about local and regional activities, write Public Relations Dept., InterVarsity Christian Fellowship, 6400 Schroeder Rd., P.O. Box 7895, Madison, WI 53707-7895.

Distributed in Canada through InterVarsity Press, 860 Denison St., Unit 3, Markham, Ontario L3R 4H1, Canada.

The Scripture quotations contained herein are from the Revised Standard Version of the Bible copyrighted 1946, 1952, 1971 by the Division of Christian Education of the National Council of the Churches of Christ in the U.S.A. and are used by permission. All rights reserved.

ISBN 0-8308-1719-0

Printed in the United States of America

Library of Congress Cataloging-in-Publication Data

McCullough, Donald W., 1949-
    Finding happiness in the most unlikely places/Donald W.
McCullough.
      p.   cm.
    Includes bibliographical references.
    ISBN 0-8308-1719-0
    1. Beatitudes—Devotional literature. 2. Happiness—Religious
aspects—Christianity. I. Title.
BT382.M385   1990
241.5'3—dc20   90-39841
                                          CIP

13	12	11	10	9	8	7	6	5	4	3	2	1
99	98	97	96	95	94	93	92	91	90			

To Karen,
and to our daughters,
Jennifer and Joy

ACKNOWLEDGMENTS

I'm grateful for those who helped with the creation of this book. Solana Beach Presbyterian Church provided a sabbatical from my pastoral responsibilities, and with this wonderful gift of time I was able to complete the first draft of the manuscript. My pastoral colleagues, Mary Graves, Barry Moller and Olive Haynes, cheerfully assumed extra burdens in my absence, leading with their usual dedication and grace. I wrote this book sustained by the sound of waves and the smell of saltwater: Sam and Betsy Reeves made available their home at St. Malo for two months of writing by the Pacific, and my parents, John and Ione McCullough, made available their home on Whidbey Island for two months of writing by Puget Sound. Ken and Shari Regan offered valuable proofreading assistance, and Marsha Mather and Susie Dysland provided excellent secretarial help. My friends at InterVarsity Press continue to be a joy to work with—especially my editor, Don Stephenson, a man of wise insight and constant encouragement (what more could a writer ask for?). And my family—Karen and Jennifer and Joy—have faithfully surrounded me with their love. For all these I thank God.

*S*eeing the crowds,
he went up on the mountain,
and when he sat down
his disciples came to him.
And he opened his mouth
and taught them, saying:
"Blessed . . ."

1

THE QUEST
FOR THE ELUSIVE
BUTTERFLY

Everyone wants to be happy. We would like to feel, in the deep-down places of our lives, a contented smile, maybe even a belly laugh. Perhaps we can't put into words what we mean by happiness, but we know the desire for it stands behind much of what we do, and we know it's not just one more thing we want, along with meaningful relationships and significant work and material possessions, but it's the Thing itself, the reason for our pursuit of everything else.

We've all had moments of happiness—coffee briskly saluting our taste buds on a frosty morning, shoes kicked off at the end of a productive day, ears warmed by peanut butter breath whispering "I love you"—moments like fragments of music promising the existence of a full symphony. We've heard enough to hum a line or two, but we can't quite remember or anticipate the full piece.

The incessant desire within us witnesses to the difference between experiencing happiness and *being* happy. Even Leonardo da Vinci, a man of stunning talent and accomplishment, lamented, "Why am I so unhappy?" And that question has been repeated at one time or another by almost everyone. We get close to happiness at times, but we can't quite reach it. It's as though we're trying to catch an elusive butterfly that constantly slips through the net of our determination.

Some feel such unrelenting sadness that their lives, as children's paint boxes in which all colors have been washed together, are nothing but dull gray. Dullness smothers them like a winter blanket.

Living in Gray

The National Institute of Mental Health estimates that seven to fifteen million Americans suffer serious depressive symptoms at any given time, and of course many more endure less acute forms of this "common cold of mental disorders."

And the incidence of depression is rising. Studies indicate that during the last two generations it has increased roughly tenfold. Whatever the causes—no doubt a complex interplay between increasing expectations and consequent disappointments—this trend indicates that many choose to travel down the wrong path in their pursuit of happiness.

Many attempt to cope with disappointments by using chemical substances. About fourteen million people in this country are alcoholics. Sixty per cent of young people age twenty-five and under have tried drugs. And Americans consume twenty-eight tons of aspirins, tranquilizers and sleeping pills *every day.*

A man recently sat in my study, near tears because of professional disappointments. He had the dishevelled look of an artist battered between his creative work and an unresponsive public. He had come to me, I suppose, because he thought he needed a sympathetic ear, maybe a spiritual pick-me-up; what he really wanted was God. Behind his quick wit and verbal dexterity was a hunger to understand how the broken pieces of his life fit together, a longing for meaning. And the odor of Scotch whiskey, as usual, was heavy on his breath though it was early in the morning. "You probably won't like my advice," I said, "but I care enough for you to speak the truth. You need to start in an Alcoholics Anonymous program."

He responded, "Well, I know I drink too much. But Pastor, what am I going to do with the sadness inside me?"

Dealing with the sadness inside isn't easy. Those who don't try to swallow or sniff short-term relief must carry on the best they can. But how? The two most common ways are to surrender or to fight; the first leads to cynicism, the second to frustration.

Surrender or Fight?

Jose Martinez has surrendered. His expectations couldn't get much lower. "We're here to die," he says, "just live and die. I drive a cab. I do some fishing, take my girl out, pay taxes, do a little reading, then get ready to drop dead. You've got to be strong about it. Life is a big fake. Nobody gives a damn. You're rich or you're poor. You're here, you're gone. You're like the wind. After you're gone, other people will come. We're gonna destroy ourselves; nothing we can do about it. The only cure for the world's illness is nuclear war— wipe everything out and start over." The voice of a realist; a man with a heart covered with concrete.

Most of us, however, would rather fight. We're not ready to let the forces of unhappiness stomp us into resigned cynicism. We still have hope; we believe that things will get better if only we can change our circumstances. So we've thrown ourselves into a desperate struggle, and what James Thurber said of Harold Ross may be true of us, too: "He lived at the corner of work and worry." Unhappiness can be a merciless whip cracking over us, pushing us into greater and greater activity. In 1973 American adults had 26.2 hours of leisure each week; in 1987 they had 16.6 hours. There never seems to be enough time to find what we're looking for. Lou Harris tells us that 86% of Americans are chronically stressed out.

Where do we think happiness will be found?

The Rich Butterfly
Some think it will be found with *money*. Money provides power to increase possessions, and possessions offer hope of damming the river of longing. Perhaps by throwing material things at the desire for happiness, the raging river will be turned into a lake of serene contentedness. So life for many of us gets reduced to a hustle, a nonsensical farce in which we buy things we don't need, at prices we can't pay, on credit we shouldn't use, with terms we can't meet, because of advertising we don't believe. We lurch from one purchase to another like drunks making a round of the bars, and the most we ever experience is a partial satisfaction that leaves us with unsatisfied thirst and the hangover of disappointment.

No one ever has enough money to buy happiness, as many have discovered after decades of trying. Of those who earn less than $15,000 a year, 5% say they have achieved the American Dream; of those who earn more than $50,000 a year, only 6% say they have achieved the American Dream.

Psychology Today conducted a survey in 1980 on the influence of money. This magazine found that people who are most money conscious (those who think about it the most, not necessarily those who have the most) are "least likely to be involved in a satisfactory love relationship." They also "report worsening health, and almost half of them are troubled by constant worry, anxiety, and loneliness."

Far from securing happiness, money often buys nothing but trouble. A friend of mine once telephoned, hoping for some sympathy. He had had a trying day, he said. He had planned to bring his boat back to Seattle from their summer place on one of the San Juan Islands. He and his wife started out in their Cadillac, but they didn't get far before it broke down. Eventually they started out again, this time in their van. Several miles later it also developed a mind of its own and decided not to cooperate. They gave up. But they hadn't been home long before the telephone rang; the renters of another house they owned were calling to complain that the refrigerator had quit working. So my friend went to fix it. While he was bent over working on the motor, the lady of the house opened a cupboard door—and forgot to shut it. As he stood to leave, he smashed his head so badly it bled like a gusher. And the next few days, of course, would have to be spent getting the two cars fixed.

Did my friend own material possessions, or did they own him? The love of money might indeed be the root of all evils, as the Good Book says, but many of us know for sure it's also the cause of headaches and ulcers.

Too bad, then, that young people forming values and planning careers haven't learned from those who have already discovered that the butterfly of wealth is as elusive as any. A recent study conducted by the Higher Education Research Institute at U.C.L.A. reports that

71% of freshman said the reason they were attending college was to make more money. (Eighteen years ago, only 39% listed personal wealth as an important goal.) Another generation seems committed to finding happiness in larger homes, nicer cars and fatter bank balances. But they will discover that you can possess enough of these things to keep an insurance agent in premiums for a lifetime and still not be happy.

The Social Butterfly

Some think happiness will be found with new *relationships*. The loneliness that in varying degrees troubles most of us becomes for some a deadly tumor gnawing their insides. They would do almost anything for relief. Read the personal want ads of almost any newspaper, and the desperation will break your heart: "40 YEAR OLD WHITE male, thin but attractive, perhaps a little too serious about life but a good sense of humor. Separated 6 months after 14 years of marriage. Enjoy reading, movies, good food, conversation, creative arguing, walking on the beach. I am able to give and receive love, but have my share of relationship fears. Not skilled at dating game. . . ." From self-advertisements like this you hear longing sharp enough to cut through the hardest pessimism, a hope that happiness will be found in a new relationship.

Given the divorce rate, you have to wonder if relationships, as enriching as they might be, ought to be the final goal toward which one should strive. Even the best marriages, for example, suffer times of loneliness and sorrow; in fact, it seems a rule of life that where the roots of love grow deepest, the risks for pain grow highest. The only people available for friendship and marriage are flawed, self-centered people like ourselves, and this, at least, ought to make us cautious. All things considered, investing one's hope for happiness in relationships is a risky business.

Few people in the latter half of the twentieth century have provoked public fascination and imagination as much as Marilyn Monroe. Though dead for many years, books about her keep rolling off the presses; pop songs about her keep hitting the top of the charts. What is it about her that still seduces? She was not the most beautiful of women; she was certainly not the most accomplished of actresses. But she has become, I think, a kind of mythological figure, a symbol of our time—restless hungering for love, unrestrained self-indulgence, bitter unfulfillment, tragic death.

During Marilyn's childhood her mother was institutionalized, and because there was no other place Marilyn could stay, she was taken to an orphanage. When she realized what was happening, she dug in her heels and yelled, "But I'm not an orphan! I'm not an orphan!" She was correct, in the factual sense, but ever after she *felt* like one and seems to have spent much of her life running from that feeling. She sought desperately to prove to the world and to herself that she wasn't unwanted, that she wasn't alone. The succession of relationships and the public adulation, however, couldn't cover the fact that, regardless of all the men who wanted her, she was fundamentally alone and unhappy.

One of the men to whom she ran was Arthur Miller, the brilliant New York playwright. The world wondered at the strange combination of this marriage: Jewish intellectual with a backslidden-fundamentalist sex kitten. But there was more to the relationship than might have been apparent from the outside. Miller's autobiography, *Timebends,* is a wonderful entrance into the heart and mind of a deeply sensitive person. He's candid about his attraction to Marilyn and his consequent frustrations and sorrows.

During the filming of *The Misfits* Miller watched her descend into the depths of depression and despair. He feared for her life as he watched their growing estrangement, her isolation from others, her paranoia, her dependence on barbiturates. One evening, after a doctor had been persuaded to give her still another shot, she was sleeping. Miller stood watching her, reflecting. "I found myself straining to imagine miracles," he writes. "What if she were to wake and I were able to say, 'God loves you, darling,' and she were to believe it! How I wished I still had my religion and she hers. . . . I had no saving mystery to offer her."

With no saving mystery and with no relationship able to pull her out of loneliness, Marilyn finally gave in to the despair and ended her life.

The Accomplished Butterfly

Some think happiness will be found with *success*. Surely the corner office, the perks of power, the sense of achievement, and honor from respected colleagues will finally net the elusive butterfly. Dag Hammarskjold, when his staff gave him a surprise party as the start of his second term as Secretary General of the United Nations, quoted a favorite verse from the Swedish poet Gunnar Ekelof: "Will the day ever come when joy is great and sorrow small?" He added his own answer: "On the day we feel we are living with a duty, well fulfilled and worth our while, on that day joy is great and we can look on sorrow as being small."

But can the fulfillment of duty, however worthwhile, really bring happiness? Isn't there always more to do? Aren't there always nagging imperfections in one's work? Aren't there always the critics and climbers ready to throw you off the ladder? As someone commented, "It's tough to climb the ladder of success, especially if you're trying to keep your nose to the grindstone, your shoulder to the wheel, your eye on the ball, and your ear to the ground." Perhaps this is one reason William James said, "The exclusive worship of the bitch-goddess success is our national disease." One thing for sure: it causes a good deal of personal dis-ease.

Dan Wakefield's first novel, *Going All the Way,* was published in 1970. The Literary Guild chose it as a Duo Main Selection, *Time* listed it as a best seller for three weeks and it sold more than 800,000 copies in paperback, with foreign rights sold to England, Italy, Sweden and Japan. The dream of a lifetime had been realized.

But Wakefield became nervous and anxious. When the book made the *Time* best-seller list, he fretted that it hadn't made the *New York Times* list; when foreign rights were sold to Italy, he brooded over why they weren't taken in France. He said, "I learned what people have testified since the beginning of time, but that no one really believes until he has the experience—success and achievement and rewards are all fine, but they do not transform you, do not bring about a state of built-in contentment or inner peace or security, much less salvation . . . I was still the same person. The novel was not The Answer to all of life's problems. I had another drink."

Left to Ourselves

All these approaches to finding happiness—money, relationships, success—have a fatal flaw in common: they leave us to ourselves. When we ourselves decide what will make us happy and we ourselves set about securing it, we are left with *only* ourselves—the very thing, whether we know it or not, from which we're trying to escape, the very thing, moreover, from which we need to escape.

Tom Wolfe's novel *The Bonfire of the Vanities* accurately depicts the selfishness which imprisons all of us. Every character—from

Sherman McCoy, an investment broker with a fourteen-room apartment on Park Avenue who sees himself as Master of the Universe, to his mistress, with whom he was involved in a hit-and-run accident, to the young prosecutor in the Bronx dreaming of glory as he works on the case, to the Harlem preacher manipulating the media's coverage of the event, to the "chow" of the criminal justice system, the everyday street thugs who keep the cops and lawyers and judges busy—every single character does and says *everything* out of self-interest, out of a hunger to Grab It Now. So the book, notwithstanding its humor and raw language, is really a stern sermon on the Old Testament text, "Vanity of vanities, says the Preacher; vanity of vanities! All is vanity" (Eccles 1:2).

But this self-centered way of living will not net for us the butterfly of happiness. All our selfish efforts to capture it, so noisy with the grunting exertion of grim determination, only scare it away. No matter how hard we try, we just can't get close enough.

So we would do well to ask ourselves whether we might be missing something important, whether we've invested our lives in the best possible way.

Forgetting the Parachute

In April 1988 the evening news reported on a skydiving photographer who had jumped from a plane in order to film other skydivers as they fell and opened their parachutes. Suddenly, as the last parachute opened, the picture on the telecast went black. The announcer reported that the cameraman had fallen to his death. It wasn't until he reached for his rip cord that he realized that he had jumped out of the plane without his parachute. So intent was he on his goal of filming the other skydivers, he neglected something crucial for saving his own life.

If we're not careful we can make the similar mistake of focusing on something we think will bring us happiness, only to discover when it's too late that we have overlooked the things that will save our lives.

Every day we all face something far riskier than skydiving: choice. We have the power to pursue certain goals and turn our backs on other goals, to invest ourselves in one way and disinvest ourselves from other ways. It's part of the glory and terror of being human. And it means we can miss our lives the way one misses a plane.

Choosing Life

The way we choose to live has to do with much more than finding happiness; it has to do with finding meaning in life. "Fear not that thy life shall come to an end," Cardinal Newman said, "but rather fear that it shall never have a beginning."

Life does not begin until we start living according to God's purposes. Just as hammers must pound, or birds must fly, or sailboats must sail—just as all things must fulfill their intended purposes to be true to themselves—even so, we must live according to the Creator's will for us to become fully human. To live differently, to follow a way of our own choosing, leads finally to the unhappiness of a forfeited life.

The unhappy world we live in indicates that many pursue the elusive butterfly on their own; they have decided for themselves what will bring fulfillment and what must be avoided. But that is like jumping out of the plane without a parachute. To neglect the Creator's intentions can at best be described as shortsighted foolishness.

How does God intend us to live? Christians believe that God has shown us in Jesus Christ. Through the man from Galilee, God has revealed the way to authentic life and thus also to happiness.

God's Way to Happiness

Whether or not one accepts the various doctrines of the Church about such things as Jesus' death and resurrection, it only makes sense to try to understand what he had to say about finding happiness in life. For nearly two millennia, millions upon millions have witnessed—often at the cost of their lives—that he spoke not simply truths but Truth, that he revealed the inner heart of all reality. Much of western culture has been built on the foundation of his teaching. What would music be without Bach? What would painting be without Rembrandt? What would literature be without Tolstoy? Now, one may finally decide that it's all a big mistake, that Jesus was wrong. But how can anyone be serious about life and the discovery of happiness without at least considering what he taught?

I know: Christians haven't always appeared very happy. I agree with Friedrich Nietzsche that "his disciples should look more redeemed," and I'm not surprised that Robert Louis Stevenson would comment, as though shocked by something unusual, "I have been to church today, and am not depressed." If there is a fountain of happiness, Christians, it often seems, haven't yet gotten their cups wet.

The reason is that they, along with everyone else, still pursue their own notions of happiness. This self-governance the Bible calls sin, and no one—not even the old saint who has devoted her entire life to worship and good works—is exempt from this affliction. Sin has marred all human life.

But Christians are those who accept God's forgiveness and commit themselves to following Jesus Christ as Lord. To the extent that they live in obedience to their Master, they're headed in the right direction; they haven't yet arrived, but they're on the road the Bible says leads to abundant life.

So the real issue isn't whether this or that person who claims to follow Jesus is any happier than others. Some are and some aren't, depending on how far down the road they happen to be. The significant question is, What did Jesus teach?

Blessedness

Jesus had some important things to say about happiness. At the start of the Sermon on the Mount (Mt 5—7), the summary of his preaching about life in the new age dawning in him, Jesus declared certain people "blessed." In speaking this way Jesus used a word familiar to both Greek and Hebrew cultures.

The Greeks had declared the gods blessed and by that referred to a transcendent happiness beyond care and death. Eventually the term was applied to humans, becoming a leading philosophical term for inner happiness.

And the Hebrews also spoke of blessedness; the beatitude became a familiar part of the practical wisdom of the Old Testament. People were declared blessed who received God's reward for righteous living.

When Jesus used the word, however, he added something new. He connected blessedness not with observations about everyday life, in the way Ben Franklin, say, noticed that "early to bed, early to rise, makes a man healthy, wealthy and wise." No, Jesus told of a blessedness not discernable in the ordinary course of things; a blessedness, in fact, coming out of a complete reversal of human values. The blessedness he announced was part of the kingdom of God—the merciful, powerful reign of God—that he himself brought to the world.

Blessed people are those who live in a new and different way because their lives have come under the control of God through the lordship of Jesus Christ. And they should be congratulated: they have found authentic happiness! So when Jesus said, for example, "Blessed are the poor in spirit," he was saying, as we will see in the next chapter, "Congratulations to the poor in spirit! They are humbly open to God's control (the kingdom), and thus will be happy in this life and the next." The happiness they experience, like the kingdom itself, is both a present and future reality; they enjoy its partial presence now and will possess its complete fulfillment in the future.

In his Beatitudes, then, Jesus shows us the way to happiness. But be forewarned: happiness is a serious business. It has nothing to do with shallow frivolity; actually, it's not easy being happy. Saul Bellow has his fictional Herzog confess, *"To tell the truth, I never had it so good . . . But I lack the strength of character to bear such joy. That was hardly a joke. When a man's breast feels like a cage from which all the dark birds have flown—he is free, he is light. And he longs to have his vultures back again. He wants his customary struggles, his nameless, empty works, his anger, his afflictions and his sins."*

Herzog might be right; there's something comfortable about our familiar patterns of finding happiness. The real thing is almost too much for us to bear, because the real thing is nothing less than the presence of God, the Joy for which every fiber of our being longs whether we know it or not.

What Jesus intends to do, then, is to get us ready for such Joy, to lead us into a way of life that prepares us for the happiness of God's presence.

Study Questions

1. In your opinion, what is success?
2. Where do you look for happiness? Explain.
3. When you look for happiness, do you find it? Explain.
4. What is the fatal flaw in trying to find happiness in money, relationships or success?
5. What is the relationship between happiness and living as God intended us to live?
6. In your opinion, what is the difference between experiencing happiness and being happy?
7. Do you think your generation is happier than your parents'? Explain.

*B*lessed are
the poor in spirit,
for theirs is the
kingdom of heaven.

2

GOOD NEWS
FOR THOSE
IN THE VALLEY

Are you content now?" the caterpillar asked Alice in Wonderland. "Well, I should like to be a *little* larger," she said. "Three inches is such a wretched height to be . . . I'm not used to it!"

We would all like to be a little larger, wouldn't we? Not necessarily taller, but larger—larger in the esteem of others, larger in feelings of personal worth, larger in influence, larger in moral integrity, larger in spiritual devotion. Three inches seems such a wretched height to be.

First Deadly Sin

We feel disgust with littleness because of pride. Pride, according to Christian tradition, is the first deadly sin. This may surprise us.

Nowadays pride assumes an honored place in the Most Admired Human Characteristics Hall of Fame. Advertisers appeal to material pride, psychiatrists massage limping pride, politicians promote national pride, civil-rights leaders cultivate racial pride, coaches incite team pride, business leaders promote civic pride, we all nurse wounded pride. What's wrong with pride?

First, a distinction. Not all pride is bad. Common sense makes room for a wholesome pride, the pride, say, a craftsman feels after months of creating an end table with perfectly joined corners and a finish you could use as a mirror. The pride of accomplishment can't be bad or God would be the first sinner; after six days of fashioning a universe, the Bible tells us, the Creator admired the result and said, "Very good." Perhaps we shouldn't even use the word *pride* in this sense. What we are really describing in this case is the pleasure of work well done. It's no sin to enjoy, with gratitude and a feeling of achievement, the fruit of careful labor—whether it be a great football team or a humane city or a magnificent universe.

The pride condemned by Scripture is altogether different, having more to do with character than creativity. It deserves to be called the first deadly sin because it describes the self-centeredness at the heart of sin. Cheating and boozing and fornicating don't make a person a sinner; these things happen as a consequence of rotating one's life around the axis of self. We were not made to inhabit the center of things. By so doing, we trespass another's territory. The serpent seduced Eve into eating forbidden fruit by saying, "You will not die. For God knows that when you eat of it your eyes will be opened, and you will be like God" (Gen 3:4-5). To be like God: that's the original temptation; to seize the center, to commandeer the throne in order to control, if not the universe, at least one's own life. Sin is the attempt, to use Dorothy Sayers's picturesque phrase, "to creep under the ribs of God." Sin *is* pride.

In a collection of children's correspondence I saw this letter from Wayne, age eleven: "Dear God, My dad thinks he is you. Please straighten him out." We all need that straightening out—for our own good. Pride leads to destructive consequences.

The Problem with Pride

Pride provokes us to seek self-worth in our achievements. Why do we run until we feel like marathoners on the last mile of the race? Why do we work until we feel as ragged as the business edge of a ripsaw? Isn't it because deep down, in those inner spaces we tend to conceal even from ourselves, we believe that if we *do* more we'll be *worth* more? By assuming control of our lives, we are left with the responsibility of justifying ourselves and establishing our own worth.

This isn't easy. When we proudly step into God's shoes we discover it's a bad fit. Only God can fulfill the functions of the center place; only God has the power to create a worth which transcends our flawed attempts to make something good out of our lives.

So along with death and taxes, failure becomes an inescapable reality for us. We can never achieve enough to set our hearts at ease. And failure points a finger at us, announcing to the world and, most of all, to us that we really aren't worth much after all. What can you do, in this case, but try to evade responsibility for botched efforts? Adam said, "She made me eat the fruit." We shift the blame by saying, "It was society's fault" or "It was improper toilet training." Anything or anyone will do, so long as we wriggle out from under failure's accusations.

When I'm irritable with my wife, angry that something hasn't gone my way, I usually apologize *and* offer an explanation (excuse).

If it weren't for the woman who took two hours of my sermon-preparation time to talk about her marital problems, I wouldn't be in such a cranky mood. And the woman, as she left my study, apologized for the interruption, but what else could she do, given the situation with her husband? And her husband, given the opportunity, would have pointed to his problems at work, especially the unreasonable demands of management. And his boss would have accounted for his behavior by telling about the attempted hostile takeover of the company. And on and on it goes, one rationalization after another, like dominoes of evasion knocking one another over with accusations.

An Accusing Voice

It would be nice if we could blame others for our problems. But it doesn't work. Eventually Wayne's dad—all of us—get straightened out. A little voice within whispers, "You're not that great. You're a big phony, acting like a Thanksgiving dinner but tasting like a cold hot dog." Sometimes we're fairly successful at silencing this voice, even when it begins to shout obscenities to an already wounded self-image, by working even harder to impress ourselves and the world. It's a vicious circle, with pride connecting every link of the chain: we seize control of our lives, we work to create our own sense of worth, we feel inadequate, we work even harder . . .

Thank God, sometimes the voice within gets too loud to ignore. Nothing can silence it—not our frenetic pace, or our can-do pep talks, or our give-yourself-a-hug-today culture, or our sessions with the psychotherapist. The voice has no respect; it behaves like an irreverent, restless child in the sanctuary of self-affirmation. Thank God, I say, when this happens, because that tiresome voice might actually be heralding the start of a new life.

The Happiness of Spiritual Poverty

The Sermon on the Mount begins with one of the most incredible sentences in the Bible: "Blessed are the poor in spirit, for theirs is the kingdom of heaven" (Mt 5:3). What a surprising thing for Jesus to say! We would expect him to say, "Blessed are the *rich* in spirit . . ." We would expect him, of all people, to declare happy those who have cultivated a powerful spirituality, who have both the gifts to help others and the inner resources to draw upon in their own time of need. But no, he proclaims happy the *dispirited* ones; he congratulates those who in the world of the spirit feel like Tijuana garbage pickers.

The Greek word for "poor" which Matthew uses comes from the verb meaning "to cower" or "to cringe." So it refers to the abject poor, not simply to those who wish they had more. It refers to those who long for *something*, to those who lack the wherewithal to cope, to those who have reached bottom spiritually and psychically, to those have tried hard—again and again!—to be better Christians but find themselves near their own end zone on fourth down with twenty-five yards to go and an injured kicker on the bench.

Being poor in spirit has nothing to do with assuming a diffident or retiring or weak personality. What is it? It is, quite simply, a lack of pride. The poor in spirit know they have lost control, should never have tried to take control, and never again want control. The poor in spirit don't at all feel like saints; they feel ineffective in prayer, and for that matter, totally unworthy of the Almighty's attention. When others testify to spiritual victories, the poor in spirit want to crawl under the pew.

And they don't exactly feel blessed. The blessedness Jesus attributed must have to do with something other than feelings. If you ask the poor in spirit how they feel, they will say, "Poor in spirit," not

"Blessed." Blessedness must refer to something more than subjective experience; it must refer to an objective state of affairs that transcends human emotions.

Why did Jesus congratulate them? Because "theirs is the kingdom of heaven." The arrangement of the words in the Greek sentence emphasizes that the kingdom exists precisely for the spiritually poor. The kingdom—the rule of God in all its life-giving, saving power—belongs to them.

A Subversive Idea

This first Beatitude is one of the most revolutionary statements ever uttered. To believe it automatically makes one a counterculture subversive. The dominant beatitude of our society is: Blessed are those who believe in themselves, for theirs is the kingdom of success. We congratulate the upbeat in spirit who take hold of life and achieve great things. This has been a significant part of the American ethos from Benjamin Franklin to Horatio Alger to contemporary preachers of positive thinking.

Some years ago I saw a headline in the sports section of the *Los Angeles Times* which read, "No Room for Losers at Ohio State." That says it all. No room for failure, no room for anything but success.

Nancy Howser, commenting in *Sports Illustrated,* said she was brought up to believe that it wasn't important whether you won or lost, but how you played the game. In the real world, however, that seemed all wrong. She learned you have to win to get anywhere in life, and it doesn't matter how you do it. So she adjusted her values to accommodate.

But then cancer attacked her husband's brain, and after two surgeries Dick had to resign as manager of the Kansas City Athletics. Things were put in a different perspective. "After what has happened," she said, "I realize that my priorities in the so-called real world were all wrong. Now Dick and I know that the old way was the right way."

The "real world" taught the Howsers they had to win to get anywhere; the trauma of brain cancer showed them the fallacy of this. Most of us, though, still live by the beatitude of triumph: Blessed are those who believe in themselves, for theirs is the kingdom of success.

But Jesus said, "Blessed are the poor in spirit." Now we can agree with him or disagree, but let's be honest about the explosive import of these words. They blow to bits the house of self-sufficiency we have built with the help of pride and the support of our surrounding culture.

Good News For Failures

For this reason these words offer comfort to those wearied by the work of self-justification and beat up by the heavy fist of failure. "The gospel of Jesus," said Reinhold Niebuhr, "is not a gospel of obvious success, but of ultimate success through obvious failure." The good news proclaimed by Jesus in this first Beatitude declares that we can honestly admit defeat in securing our own worth, admit that spiritually we haven't got a dime to our name—and that this admission opens us to the kingdom of God.

Jesus congratulated the poor in spirit because they know just how needy they really are; they know it's time to move over and let God take control; they know they are absolutely dependent on the grace of God. They are the blessed ones, because this helplessness is the first—and only—requirement for receiving God's help.

The first necessity for a proper relationship with God is not "accepting Jesus," or getting baptized, or joining a church, or doing a good deed. These things come from something more fundamental; they grow out of the soil of humility. "It is worth remembering that the root of the words *humiliation* and *humility* is humus." We meet God more often in the manure of failure than on the mountain of success.

In Nikos Kazantzakis's novel *Christ Recrucified* there is a scene in which four men are confessing their sins to one another in the presence of a pope (the term for pastor in the Greek Orthodox Church). One of them, Manolios, who is to play the part of Christ in the village passion play, shudders at his unworthiness. He admits to seeing the widow Katerina at the well. Her lips were made up, and her bodice was open enough for him to see her breasts. The blood rose to his head; he was giddy with desire for her. The only thing that kept him from hurling himself upon her was fear—fear of what people would think, fear of God.

But one evening he could hold out no longer. He started walking to the widow's house. He told himself that he was going to save her soul, to lead her in the way of God. But he knew what he was really doing: he was rushing to sleep with her. Lust had overwhelmed him and he had given in to his craving.

But on the way a strange thing happened. The flesh of his face swelled into a hideous mask, as though God had mercifully intervened by covering him with a repulsive wound.

The friends sat in silence, transfixed with terror. "Shuddering, they felt that God besieges each one of us, like a lion. Sometimes you feel his breath, hear his roaring, see his eyes piercing the darkness."

And then Michelis cries out, "How can God let us live on the earth? Why doesn't He kill us to purify creation?" And the pope answers, "Because, Michelis, God is a potter; He works in mud."

The pope might have said that God works *only* in mud. Those who pridefully try to lift themselves out of the mud by their own efforts only frustrate the work of the artist. The first Beatitude is first for a reason: it reaffirms the grace of God which precedes everything else. The heart of the gospel proclaimed by Jesus and his apostles is that God graciously lifts those who cannot lift themselves.

So Jesus congratulated the poor in spirit. Having given up on their own power, they are ready for the power of God. "Theirs is the kingdom of heaven." In the language of the Gospels, "kingdom" refers to God's reign, to the sovereign exercise of grace over sin, the royal gift of life in place of death. When rebellious pride lays down its arms, God's power invades to save.

Grace in the Valley

The Sermon on the Mount begins in the valley. The first sentence addresses those who feel low . . . very low. Every sentence which follows refers back to the good news of grace for those who have hit rock bottom. It's as if Jesus said, "Look, here's a great mountain you need to climb as my disciple. The sermon you're about to hear will show you the kind of life expected of my people. But you must first realize that you cannot climb this mountain. Don't even try to take the first step out of the valley until you understand this. Being a kingdom person means living by God's power, not by your power. So if you feel as spiritually destitute as a bag lady wandering city streets, cheer up! You're more blessed than you think. God has a thing for poor bag ladies; God fills where he first finds emptiness."

Rembrandt's great painting of the woman caught in adultery conveys the essence of this first Beatitude. The artist's use of light, as in many of his works, reveals the truth of the gospel. All light flows from Christ, the tallest figure on the canvas. The men near him, upright in self-righteousness and judgmental attitudes, stand in shadows. The sinful woman is lowest of all; she alone kneels with head bowed, poor in spirit. But the light of Christ bathes her, surrounds her with splendor. She receives grace through humility. Hers is the kingdom of heaven.

Study Questions

1. How would you distinguish between good and bad pride?
2. Cite both good and bad examples of pride.
3. What does it mean to be poor in spirit?
4. The author maintains that we congratulate the positive in spirit who hold onto life rather than the poor in spirit. How do you see this happening in our society?
5. Why is it so hard to admit utter helplessness to God?
6. What do the "poor in spirit" have going for them in relation to God?

*B*lessed are
those who mourn,
for they shall be
comforted.

3

IN PRAISE
OF GRIEF

With this second Beatitude, Jesus uttered one of the strangest sentences imaginable. What sense does it make to declare happy those who are sad? *We* would congratulate those with eyes lined by laughter; Jesus congratulates those with eyes flooded by grief. *We* would congratulate those with mirth in their hearts; Jesus congratulates those with an ache in their guts. What sense does this make?

Very little, if we share the values of our culture.

A few years ago Russell Baker commented that

the number of places a person can escape entertainment becomes smaller every year. . . . It used to be, for example, that a man could go to his dentist and count on an undisturbed bout of suffering which helped him to grasp the transience of life and perceive the agony of the flesh. No longer. Nowadays, while the drill bites at his nerve ends, he will be entertained by an invisible orchestra playing 'The March of the Wooden Soldiers' through a hole in the ceiling. The invisible orchestra is spreading across the country like the chestnut blight. . . . A people forced to live with Leonard Bernstein in the elevator, Doris Day at 30,000 feet, and 'The Animals' on the commuter bus is a people that will have precious little to smile about at the end of a hard-day's entertainment. To restore entertainment to its proper role in society, we must restore the right to brood undisturbed.

And, I would add, we must restore the right to be sad. The stampede toward entertainment begins, so often, with the flight from sorrow. Better to have something pleasant distract us, we might think, than have something painful destroy us. Too many hurts seem ready to ambush our emotions and beat them senseless if given half a chance. So off to the movies or the mall, the boat or the ball game, the pool or the party—off to almost anything at all promising protection from sadness and the possibility of happiness.

If we're beating our hooves in this stampede, we've defined happiness much too narrowly. Authentic happiness doesn't mean absence of sorrow. In fact, Jesus said, "Blessed are those who mourn."

Mourning, Not Moaning

Mourning: Jesus wasn't referring to the sadness I feel, say, when the Padres lose three straight games, or when a patrolman pulls me over and my fast-talking preacher-mouth can't get me out of a speeding ticket; he wasn't even referring to the sadness I feel when I've hurt my wife's feelings, or when I've been short-tempered with my daughters. I feel bad about these things, but I don't mourn.

The word used here is the strongest in the Greek language. It's used for mourning the dead, for the passionate lament of a broken heart. Intense sorrow. "Happy are the mourners," Jesus said.

Happy are the mourners, not the moaners. Some find pleasure in complaining. "Nobody knows the trouble I've seen," they sing, and they enjoy the effect their music has on others. They like the attention; they wallow in the concern of others. But they are manipulators, more to be pitied than congratulated. Moaners are too content with their shallow pleasures to move into deep happiness.

But the mourners will be happy, according to Jesus. Why? We wouldn't expect this. After all, mourners have had a great hurt penetrate them; a sharp suffering has lanced their spirits, leaving a gaping wound to bleed grief all over their lives. Why are *they* the blessed ones? How could anyone consider them worthy of congratulation?

Sensitive Hearts

The first and obvious thing we can say about mourners is that they have enough sensitivity to hurt. That in itself deserves praise.

It's not easy to escape the conspiracy to save us from suffering. A host of saviors wait to serve us: psychologists to numb our neuroses and pastors to absolve our guilt, doctors to heal our diseases and insurance agents to calm our worries, the Surgeon General to save our lungs and Jane Fonda to remove our flab. And we're separated from the suffering of others, too, by comfortable neighborhoods to protect our families, hospitals to care for the sick and funeral homes to tend the dead. Deliverance from discomfort may be the most bullish industry in contemporary America. A team of people, like maintenance workers at Disneyland, are quick to sweep the garbage out of our lives to make our visit to the Magic Kingdom as pleasant as possible as we go from one entertainment to another.

But Jesus congratulated those who have left the Magic Kingdom to enter God's Kingdom.

When the poor in spirit, having given up on themselves and their pathetic attempts to find happiness, turn in humility toward God, they discover they have been seized—wholly seized—by the grace of God. Because the *grace* of God holds them, they are liberated from guilt, but because the grace of *God* holds them, they are imprisoned anew, held captive by the good will of God. The King pardons and controls.

Kingdom people, therefore, mourn. God transforms their values and changes their perspectives. They can't live under God's authority in a sinful world without mourning. As their hearts begin beating in rhythm with God's heart, their hearts also begin breaking over the things that break God's heart.

And the paradox is this: great mourners are great rejoicers. In opening the door to pain, they also open it to joy. People who do not mourn, who slam the door on all sorrow, never feel the deepest delights. Their lives, like freeways on which they speed from one entertaining distraction to another, are too hard for anything but the most superficial pleasures to pass over. But those sensitive enough to be crushed by sadness are those who also can be lifted by happiness.

Surely few have grieved as deeply as Mother Theresa over the wretched poor on the streets of Calcutta. But what do visitors to her Home for the Dying report? Do they not testify to joy so authentic, so palpable, that words of description drop like arrows falling short of a target? Do they not struggle to speak of a radiance shining forth in the midst of the darkness, piling adjective on top of adjective, until finally they give up with a sigh filled with the inexplicable experience of something from another world? The great grievers, I'm convinced, are the great rejoicers, for opening eyes in the night has enabled them to see clearly the shafts of light breaking through to harass the darkness.

As a pastor, I've had the privilege and pain of sitting with families in anguish over the death of a loved one. I have often witnessed the unlikely marriage of tears and laughter. We'll be seated in the living room, say, planning Bill's funeral. The silence of sorrow surrounds each sentence. "Why did he have to die so young," Sharon says. "With two little children, with so much of a future ahead of us?" And maybe I mutter something to the new widow, or maybe I just cry with her.

Then George, who has just flown in from Denver to be with his sister, after a blast from his nose that might very well have raised Bill himself from the mortician's table, says, "If I'd known there were this many tears in the world, I'd have bought stock in the damn Kleenex company." Silence follows, for about two seconds; no one's too sure how to respond, given the circumstances and the minister's presence. But then, a snicker from one of the kids. It's enough. Like bubbles rising from the bottom of a kettle sitting long over the fire, the laughter rises to the surface until the whole room boils over with mirth far out of proportion to the humor in the comment.

A release of tension, of course. But I think more, too, as I see Sharon's eyes: she's looking at her big brother—the boy who had tried to force-feed a lizard down her screaming throat, the teen-ager who had begged for her help when he was going down for the third time in a sea of algebra, the college student who telephoned (collect) once a week for no reason other than he missed her, and the young man who had cried like a baby at her wedding—her big brother who wishes he'd bought stock in the damn Kleenex company, her big brother whom she loves with an ache almost as great as the ache in her heart because of her husband's death.

Who can understand the strange union of grief and joy in a moment such as this? Sorrow pierces the soul, cuts through protective defenses, leaves feelings exposed, vulnerable . . . and joy slips in.

"Blessed are those who mourn." Congratulations to them, for they have sensitive hearts.

Children of God

Now let's take it a step further. Mourners feel something more than a passing sorrow for events which remain external to them; mourners have allowed pain to penetrate their lives. For this reason, they show they are children of God.

Not every sad thing causes me to mourn. Some things pass over my life like rainwater over oilskin, without soaking into my being. The evening news tells me of a flood in Bangladesh, a mass murder in a schoolyard, and a terrifying increase in AIDS, and I shake my head over the tragedies of life. But then, without so much as a moment's reflection, I go into the kitchen for a cup of coffee, on the way tickling my daughter and asking my wife if she picked up the dry cleaning. For the most part, this may be fine; a person, after all, couldn't function if every tragedy pierced the heart.

Mourning, though, is different. I grieve deeply when something penetrates deeply. When I sat next to Garth's bedside, for example, I mourned. My normal defenses were no match for this tragedy, though God knows I would have preferred to keep a professional distance. But there's no such protection when it's your cousin's son lying there with head smashed and swollen because a drunk driver ran into a car full of Westmont College students on their way to a mission project. I had just told his parents, who were waiting to board a flight from Seattle to San Diego, that no life remained in their firstborn's brain, and I had promised to stay with him until they arrived. So I did. That's what destroyed the professional distance—sitting there, hour by hour, next to the pumping and wheezing technology of an Intensive Care Unit and next to the silence of God, too, as I wondered why such things have to happen. There was plenty of time to think. I remembered how his mother and I had played together as kids, and how his father had been in my wedding, and how I had been the first to suggest his name and how his dad had told me, just months before, how pleased he was that his son loved the Lord. And I mourned.

I didn't really feel all that blessed. But according to Jesus I was. Why? Because when we mourn in this way, when hurt slices through us like a woodsman's ax, we are being true to our heritage as children of God.

Jesus Christ, according to the witness of the Church, revealed the character of God; in the apostle's words, "in him all the fullness of God was pleased to dwell" (Col 1:19). What the Father has shown through sending the Son is a divine being, not safely separated, but profoundly pierced by the suffering of the world. So we see Jesus weeping over the death of his friend Lazarus; we see Jesus filled with compassion—com-passion—suffering with the sick and dying; we see Jesus taking the sadness of the entire world into himself and dying of a broken heart on a Roman cross. "A man of sorrows, acquainted with grief."

"Blessed are those who mourn." Congratulations to them, because they are like Christ, because they prove themselves to be children of the God who mourns.

From Tears to Action
Mourners, like Jesus Christ himself, are more likely to become in-

struments of God's healing in this world; they may transform their tears into action. Behind every hospital and hospice and food bank and school and social-service agency was someone who grieved over a human need—grieved deeply enough to do the hard work of making a difference.

Martin Luther mourned the Church's erosion of simple faith in the grace of God; John Wesley mourned his contemporaries' lack of disciplined piety; William Wilberforce mourned the slave trade; William and Catherine Booth mourned the conditions of the poor in London; Albert Schweitzer mourned the suffering of Africans; Dietrich Bonhoeffer mourned the Church's captivity to Naziism; Martin Luther King, Jr., mourned racial prejudice; Candy Lightner mourned the death of her daughter and formed MADD—Mothers Against Drunk Driving.

"Blessed are those who mourn." Congratulations to them, because they may hurt enough to do something about it.

God at the Broken Places

Happy are the sad? I've suggested several reasons why mourners are blessed. They have sensitive hearts, they prove themselves children of God and their tears may be turned into healing action. But there's a more important reason, the one Jesus gave: "Blessed are those who mourn, for they shall be comforted" (Mt 5:4).

Comforted by whom? Comforted by God.

God comes to the brokenhearted in a way that sustains and renews. Karl Barth introduced a section of his *Church Dogmatics* with these words: "We must begin by saying something about the nature of the man who is in some sense illuminated by the light of the kingdom of God. What kind of man is it to whom Jesus turns in this particular activity? The answer is obvious. It is the man with whom things are going badly; who is needy and frightened and harassed. . . . The picture brought before us is that of suffering—the demon possessed, the relatives of a sick friend who is dear to them, the bereaved and those who walk in the fear and shadow of death."

Jesus turns to the one for whom things are going badly. I have witnessed this, again and again; I have seen, coming from those in crushing grief, surprising peace and even startling joy.

The first time I saw Al outside of church was at the beach. I had just run about six miles and had the raised chin and easy stride of a man clearly in charge of the world. Good pace, I told myself. Pretty Hot Stuff.

And then a voice brought me out of my silent self-admiration: "Hi Pastor! Great day for a run!" I looked up to see a trim, sweat-soaked, white-haired man in his mid-sixties.

"Well, Al," I responded, "I didn't know you're a runner." That's what I said, but this is what I thought: How wonderful for an old guy like you to be out getting a little exercise. Pretty Hot Stuff pulled in his stomach and made sure he wasn't breathing too hard. "How far have you run today, Al?"

"Eighteen miles," he said.

"I beg your pardon?"

"Eighteen. I'm doing a lighter one today. It's my training schedule. I'm getting ready for another marathon. How far you going today?"

I muttered something about a sore calf, and limped away—not from a wounded muscle but from a chastened spirit.

Al became my hero. Whenever I ran he came to mind; by God's grace, I wanted to grow up to be just like him. Running eighteen miles at sixty-five! The very thought of it lightened my feet and enlarged my lungs.

Then one day the receptionist buzzed me on the intercom. Al had stopped by, she told me. Did I have a few minutes to chat? A man always has time for his hero, so I told her to send him up right away.

"Uh . . . well . . ." she faltered. "Perhaps you had better come downstairs."

When I saw Al seated I sensed something was wrong. He didn't look quite right, and I felt my spirit sinking even before he reached out and said, "Pastor, can you help me up? My legs aren't working very well."

His weight bearing down on me, as we hobbled down the hallway like two hopeless runners in a gunnysack race, was nothing compared with the weight dragging my spirit onto the floor. How could this be? In a way, I felt some of my own dreams being crippled with each halting step we made.

But then his words lifted me and held me, and to this day they hold me still and keep me . . . well, if not flying with eagles at least walking without fainting. What he said was this: "Pastor, about a month ago I noticed myself slowing down on my run. Things have happened rapidly since then. The neurologist says I have A.L.S.— Lou Gehrig's disease. I don't know how long I have to live.

"But you know, Pastor, God is good. I feel such peace. It's incredible. I've never felt closer to God. I know my life is in my Savior's hands, and I'm ready for whatever he has for me."

"Blessed are those who mourn," Jesus said, "for they shall be comforted." That's what Al had: the comfort of God.

And that's what Frank felt, too. Just hours after a highway patrolman told him that his twenty-year-old daughter had been killed on the freeway, he looked up at me and said, "Don, I don't like it. I'm mad. I don't understand why God would allow this to happen. She was on her way home from helping lead a Young Life Club! I don't understand! I will never understand. But Don, it's going to be all right." And then once more, with tears streaming down his cheeks and his voice raised as if he was speaking past me and his wife, Joan, and past his own anger and doubt to some place behind it all where the company of heaven was bearing witness: "IT'S GOING TO BE ALL RIGHT!"

"Blessed are those who mourn," Jesus said, "for they shall be comforted." Simply put, it's better to mourn, to have your heart ripped out and stomped to bits by the spiked boots of tragedy, than never to mourn and miss this comfort. The God revealed through Jesus Christ and present in the power of the Holy Spirit comes to the broken places and holds the loose ends together with his powerful love. He comes, I say. He comes.

Mary Magdalene has been one of the most maligned women in history. Popular tradition holds that she was a prostitute. Pope Gregory the Great (sixth century A.D.) started the rumor when he decided she was the woman caught in adultery whom Jesus saved from death, and his opinion stuck to her like a bad reputation. But there is absolutely no scriptural evidence for this.

We do know, however, that she had the courage of a great mourner. A faithful disciple to the end, she followed Jesus to the Passover celebration in Jerusalem and mourned as he was hauled before the authorities on charges of blasphemy and sedition. She mourned as the wretched procession marched outside the city gates and up the skull-shaped hill. She mourned when the nails sunk deeply into his flesh. She mourned when he cried out in agony. Peter and the others couldn't handle it; they ran for safety, ran from the horror of it; back to tax collecting and fishing, back to families and homes. *But Mary stayed with her grief.*

So to the tomb she went early that morning, simply to be there, as a widow goes to the garage and runs her fingers across an abandoned workbench . . . remembering; or as a father sits in an empty bedroom trying somehow to fill an aching emptiness within, remembering. Through the dark, empty streets outside the gates to Jesus' tomb, to continue her work of mourning.

She stayed with her grief, I tell you, and didn't run from it; she let herself be drawn into the pain and tragedy of Jesus' death.

Do you know the end of the story? To whom did the resurrected Lord first appear on Easter morn? Who felt the Comforting Presence before anyone else? Mary. Mary, who stayed with her grief until the comfort came. Blessed Mary.

IN PRAISE OF GRIEF

Study Questions

1. Do you think we live in an entertainment-oriented culture? Why or why not?
2. What is the difference between happiness and the absence of sorrow?
3. Explain the difference between mourners and moaners.
4. What is the relationship between mourners and God's grace?
5. Cite an example of a way in which you have experienced God's grace?
6. Give an example of great joy that you have felt during an especially sad time in your life. Would the joy have been as great without the accompanying sadness?
7. According to Jesus, why are we blessed when we mourn?
8. How can mourners become instruments of healing?
9. Why is the mourner closer to God than the non-mourner?

*B*lessed are
the meek,
for they shall
inherit the earth.

4

THE STRENGTH
OF GENTLENESS

George Steinbrenner, owner of the New York Yankees, said, "I want this team to win. I'm obsessed with winning, with discipline, with achieving. That's what this country's all about."

Yes, this country honors winners; rewards go to the competitive, the ones who push harder and stay longer, the ones who play the games of power and come out on top. So we teach our children to assert themselves, to settle for nothing less than president of the student council or first chair in the trumpet section or acceptance by a prestigious university. And what we want for them often reflects what we have wanted for ourselves, the striving that may or may not have won for us the satisfaction of achievement, the pleasure of victory. The early bird may get the worm, but if you had something other than worms in mind, if you prefer salmon, say, then you had better learn to fly with the eagles. Admiration from others, rewards for work well-done, financial comfort, invitations into the best social circles—these things don't just happen. They come after flying high and diving deep. Blessed are the aggressive, we believe, for they shall inherit the earth.

But on the way up the ladder of success, we just might bump into Jesus who always seems to be on the way down. And what he has to say will startle us; by God's grace, it may even save us.

The Price We're Paying

If what Jesus had to say about finding happiness is true, or even if it's *possibly* true, we had better pay careful attention to him. For aggressiveness has costly consequences. Judith Lechman has indicated that "two hundred seventy people are being killed by other human beings during every hour of each day. Unaccountable others are being unjustly imprisoned, tortured, or held hostage worldwide. Approximately thirty-three thousand men, women, and children each month slip below the subsistence level, succumbing to disease, starvation, and, ultimately, death. Meanwhile, our participation in the well-documented pollution of our land, oceans and air continues with unabated selfishness." In the struggle to get to the top many people get mashed on the bottom. If there is another way to happiness, we should at least consider it before our world and nation and families—indeed, we ourselves—completely fall apart because of self-centered aggressiveness.

Meekness, Not Weakness

"Blessed are the meek," Jesus said, "for they shall inherit the earth" (Mt 5:5).

Meekness. Let's admit it: we don't like the word. It tastes insipid, smells like morning-mouth, and looks like Caspar Milquetoast; it has the strength of a cooked noodle. Coaches don't rally teams with it; executives don't send sales people into the field with it; politicians don't promise to lead by it; parents don't counsel children to develop it; generals don't embolden troops with it. You won't find anyone offering seminars on meekness training. It probably should be examined by the House Committee on Un-American Activities.

Or so we think.

Actually, the Greek word rendered "meek" is tough to translate. No single word in our language quite holds together its nuances. But if we had to select one word to convey its meaning it would have to be *gentle.* A meek person, the way the Bible uses the word, is a gentle person. "Blessed are gentlemen and gentlewomen."

Gentleness is a relational term. It has to do with our relationships with ourselves and others.

Being Gentle with Ourselves

Often our self-centered aggressiveness comes from not liking ourselves very much. Insecurities push us to prove to others and, most of all, to ourselves that we have value; if only we could get to the top of the ladder of success, we might think, surely we would feel more worthwhile.

Though I watch little television, I was saddened when the Muppets went off the air. Enjoying Kermit and the gang had become a Saturday-night ritual in our home. My favorite, of course, was Miss Piggy. So when she published her book, *Miss Piggy's Guide to Life,* I wasted no time in buying my own copy.

"In a word," she writes, "beauty is being yourself." Yes, I thought, this is my kind of pig. But then the bacon went rancid on me. With every succeeding sentence she revealed her own insecurities, her own intense desire to convince herself of her own beauty: "Yes, there is a terrible pressure that comes with being the object of so much attention, of so many adoring fans, but there is also the satisfaction of providing your public with a vision of true beautology, true stylisity—how can I put it?—true glamorositude, in a world that can sometimes seem, well, a little on the gray side." But does her public ever see what she wants them to see? Apparently not: "Never forget that only you can ever fully appreciate your own beauty. Others may try but they so often fall short."

Poor Miss Piggy. And poor Phyllis Diller. Since 1971 when she was fifty-four, she has had two face lifts (a major and a mini), two nose-jobs, a tummy tuck, a breast reduction, three teeth bondings, a forehead and an under-eye lift, an eyeliner tattoo, cheek implants and a chemical peel. (What is a chemical peel?) "After each surgery," she declares, "I like myself better and so do the men in my life." True glamorositude, I suppose.

And this plastic, pathetic attempt to create self-worth is paralleled in countless ways by men and women who play water-cooler politics to get the corner office, and gossip their way into the right group, and leverage themselves into a fat portfolio, and who, in order to get their kids on top of the pile before they're even aware there *is* a pile, start teaching them Spanish conversation and French cooking and Suzuki violin before they're out of pre-school.

The meek are more gentle with themselves. It's not that they forsake all efforts at self-improvement. But their aspirations and achievements flow out of a relaxed center. They basically accept themselves as they are, and therefore do not have to prove their worth by coming out on top; they have, to risk using a cliché, a positive self-image.

The Source of Our Worth

How does this self-relationship come about? Some seek it at the top of the ladder of achievement, as I've said, and others seek it in a positive-thinking seminar or on a psychotherapist's couch. These approaches provide, at best, temporary relief. We need something more fundamental—something that can crown our lives with an unfading honor able to withstand the ravages of failure and the accusations of guilt. We need, in other words, an eternal worth.

Only God can confer such worth. And according to Scripture, God has. In Ephesians we read, "I beg you to lead a life worthy of the calling to which you have been called, with all lowliness and meekness . . ." (4:1-2); similarly, in Colossians we are exhorted to "put on then, as God's chosen ones . . . meekness" (3:12). In both these passages the apostle connects meekness with the electing grace of God.

We can be gentle with ourselves when we realize we have been called, not because of our accomplishments or personal goodness, but because of a searching, claiming grace revealed in Jesus Christ. God has adopted us, made us part of a family bound together by bonds of eternal love. We have worth, therefore, an unfading honor independent of what the world may think; it's ours whether we win, lose or tie; it's ours whether we come out on top of the heap or find ourselves suffocating at the bottom.

God has chosen us, lifted us to an eternal glory, and that necessarily means we are God's. The meek realize this. Dietrich Bonhoeffer said the meek "renounce every right of their own and live for the sake of Jesus Christ. When reproached, they hold their peace; when treated with violence they endure it patiently; when men drive them from their presence, they yield their ground. . . . They are determined to leave their rights to God alone. . . . Their right is the will of their lord—that and no more."

So the meek are non-defensive. Why should they try to protect themselves? They are God's. They have no need to vindicate themselves. G. K. Chesterton once quipped that "angels can fly because they take themselves so lightly." Well, the meek can soar. They enjoy freedom from constant self-criticism. God alone will judge them, and the Judge is merciful beyond comprehension. In this freedom they can be open to new ideas and open to others.

Being Gentle with Others

Because the meek are controlled by God, they have no need to control others. They know they have been given eternal worth. What need have they to manipulate others into giving them temporal worth?

Besides, God has called these others, too, and secured their worth through Jesus Christ, and thus they have a right to their own uniqueness. The meek grant others this space; they know God reigns and can manage things very nicely without their assistance.

When I forget God is in control of things, I'm more likely to struggle to maintain my own control of people and events in my life. One of the most challenging responsibilities for a Presbyterian pastor is moderating the session—the ruling board of a congregation. We have twenty-five elders and pastors comprising our session, and that sometimes means twenty-five different ideas about how the church ought to be run.

I prepare for these meetings like General Eisenhower preparing for the invasion of Europe. On the day of the meeting I try to leave my office a couple of hours early in order to run along the beach, take a long shower, and listen to a recording of my beloved Bach. I talk to God through all this, offering my recommendations on how things ought to go that evening. But I've learned to talk with myself, too. The conversation goes something like this:

"Self," I say, "whose church is this, anyway?"

"God's," I answer.

"And who called the elders and pastors to serve on the session?"

"God."

"And who has been running creation for millions of years before you were born and won't have any problem carrying on when you die?"

"God."

"Self, are you getting the point?"

"I think so," I say.

And then I ask God to help me remember. When I do, I'm more relaxed with others, gentler. In the midst of a hot discussion in which comments whiz through the room like bullets from automatic weapons and my passions heat up and my desire to win intensifies, I remind myself that the church isn't mine. It's God's. And I remind myself, further, that if the session makes a dumb decision it will be God's problem to fix! After all, *my* glory isn't at stake. At that point I can step back with what I like to think of as a sanctified nonchalance; I'm able to lead without manipulating, to guide without pounding opponents into the floor, to moderate without having to win.

More Tolerant

Not only does an awareness of our dependence on the grace of God free us from the burden of controlling others, it frees us from the burden of judging others. The meek are tolerant, less judgmental.

I don't mean to imply that the meek never discriminate between good and evil, that in a wishy-washy way they nod approval to all things. No: the meek, being under the control of God, also mourn—

grieve deeply over the sins of the world. But because they know they have been claimed by God's grace in Jesus Christ, they also know that *in essence* they are no better than anyone else. The apostle Paul confessed, "I am the foremost of sinners" (1 Tim 1:15). The only thing setting him apart from anyone else, he believed, was a summons and a commission he didn't deserve; he was utterly dependent on God. So the worst sinner became the foremost preacher of grace.

Having received God's mercy, the meek offer it to others.

When I was at that age when a car could raise as much lust in me as women could in later years, when I was old enough to think I knew how to drive but young enough not to be able to drive, I happily volunteered to wash the family car. The whole point, of course, was to be able to drive it: the car was never quite in the right place in relation to the hose, and so I drove it back and forth over about fifteen feet of driveway.

I had the unhappy fortune one day to have backed over the bucket just as my father came out of the house. Neither of us can remember what was on his mind. But now that I, too, am a pastor, I can guess: a member of the church, probably, had been rushed to the hospital, or he had been called to make peace in a family dispute, or a deacon had just telephoned to criticize him about something—no doubt something like this had filled and troubled his mind when he shot through the back door . . . a Man with a Mission.

A squashed bucket under the axle he didn't need. I hadn't hurt the car. The bucket was only bent. No big deal, or so I thought. But Dad erupted in uncharacteristic anger.

"Dumb kid! Why don't you watch what you're doing! Give me the keys!"

And then he jumped into the driver's seat, started the engine, threw it into reverse, and backed out of the driveway . . . right into the neighbor's car.

I did not laugh. I wanted to. Never in my life had I wanted to laugh more—not during church when Danny farted during the pastoral prayer, not when Cousin Bob drove the pickup through the wall of Uncle Harold's barn, not when we tied Aunt Pearl's underwear in knots—never had I so wanted to let out the inner, volcanic pressure. But I did not laugh. I might have been careless with buckets, but I wasn't stupid.

When I finally had the courage to mention the incident twenty years later, we both had a good laugh. Now he's the first to admit the obvious: had he known he was about to smash into the neighbor's Chevy, he wouldn't have been upset that I ran over a bucket.

The meek remember their own vulnerabilities; they don't kid themselves into thinking they're any more than a millimeter away from disaster most of the time. But the grace of God . . . the grace of God. So they ease up on others. When they might have good reason to lash out in anger, they embrace with forgiveness; when they might be understandably irritated, they're surprisingly calm.

"Blessed are the meek." Congratulations to those who rest secure in the merciful call of God. They will be gentle with themselves and gentle with each other. Such gentleness will lead to happiness.

Great Strength

It should be clear by now that meekness, biblically understood, has nothing to do with weakness. In fact, gentleness takes great strength. A gentle person has the strength to accept himself or herself, the strength to resist the temptation to control others, and most of all, the strength to trust the grace of God.

A gentle person enjoys inner freedom and peace, and freedom and peace are like iron in the creation of character.

Consider Moses. The Old Testament tells us that "the man Moses was very meek, more than all men that were on the face of the earth" (Num 12:3).

Why was Moses meek? Because he had a very accurate view of himself. Yes, he had been called to a position of significant leadership. But the verb is crucial: he had been *called*. He hadn't even made it onto the first rung of the ladder of success when God tapped him on the shoulder; in fact, Moses was sure God had the wrong man. He was a murderer who had fled from Egypt, and for years he had been doing nothing more than herding sheep out in the desert. As for natural leadership abilities, he wouldn't have been elected secretary of the Midian Rotary Club; speaking to sheep was one thing, but talking with groups of people any larger than his wife and son gave him the shivers. No one would have elected Moses to lead the Israelites out of Egyptian bondage. No one, that is, but God.

God had chosen him, and so he could afford to be gentle with himself and others. Moses was meek.

But not weak. In his meekness he withstood the Pharaoh of Egypt, engineered the Israelite escape from slavery and led the unruly band for forty years in the wilderness. Frederick Buechner writes,

Whenever Hollywood cranks out a movie about him, they always give the part to somebody like Charlton Heston with some fake whiskers glued on. The truth of it is he probably looked a lot more like Tevye the milkman after ten rounds with Mohammed Ali.

Forty years of tramping around the wilderness with the Israelites was enough to take it out of anybody. When they weren't raising hell about running out of food, they were raising it about running out of water. They were always hankering after the flesh-pots of Egypt and making bitter remarks about how they should have stayed home and let well enough alone. As soon as his back was turned, they started whooping it up around the Golden Calf, and when somebody stood up and said he ought to be thrown out, the motion was seconded by thousands. Any spare time he had left after taking care of things like that he spent trying to persuade God not to wipe them out altogether as they deserved. The meekest man on the face of the earth was a tough old bird.

And consider Jesus. "Take my yoke upon you," he said, "and learn from me; for I am gentle and lowly in heart, and you will find rest for your souls" (Mt 11:29). The word *gentle* comes from the same Greek word that has been translated "meek" in this Beatitude. Jesus was a meek Messiah.

So he rode into Jerusalem, not on the white steed of an aggressive conqueror, but on a lowly donkey. He had no need to impress, no need to force his ideas of the kingdom. He knew who he was: a servant, called by God. He passed through the city gates in a spirit of gentleness.

No one, however, could accuse him of weakness. The day after his palm-strewn entry into Jerusalem, he visited the Temple. He saw the injustices of moneychangers taking advantage of the poor, and the righteous anger of God burned hot within him. Like Matt Dillon dealing with drunken cowboys in the Longbranch Saloon, Jesus overturned tables and physically threw out those who were trying to make a quick buck at the expense of others.

And no one could accuse him of weakness as he stood before Pilate. He was quiet, yes; he did not defend himself, true. But there was all the strength of God in his gentleness. Dale Bruner has referred to his meekness as "the poise of faith." He knew the leaders of Israel had demanded his death, and he knew the fist of Rome was about to crush him in all its terrifying ugliness—he knew this, yet he faced it with quiet courage. He felt no need to make excuses, or defend his honor, or save his life. He had been called by God and would leave his defense to God. That's the strength of holy gentleness.

The Coming Revolution

"Blessed are the meek," Jesus said. Blessed? Well, yes. I think of all the blessings Jesus declared, I best understand the logic of this one. To be at peace with oneself and others would be an obvious joy. The meek deserve congratulations, for they are at least on the way toward happiness.

Yet there is another reason why the meek are blessed, according to Jesus. "Blessed are the meek, for they shall inherit the earth." Inherit the earth? We might expect them eventually to gain heaven, but the earth?

Two things should be said about this astonishing promise. First, God is not finished with the earth. Christian hope does not look forward to an escape into heaven but to the transformation of earth. "Thy Kingdom *come*," we pray. And, in Bonhoeffer's words, "when the kingdom of heaven descends, the face of the earth will be renewed. . . . God does not forsake the earth: he made it, he sent his Son to it and on it he has built his Church. Thus a beginning has already been made in this present age. . . . The renewal of the earth begins at Golgotha, where the meek one died, and from there it will spread. When the kingdom finally comes, the meek shall possess the earth."

The second thing to note about this promise is, I suppose, obvious: a great change is coming. A revolution will take place so far exceeding anything the world has hitherto experienced that you could take the French Revolution and the American Revolution and the Russian Revolution, put them all together and that Big Revolution still wouldn't look like anything more serious than a pack of Cub Scouts unhappy that the cupcakes ran out—when compared with the upheaval that's on its way.

When the kingdom of God comes in fulfillment, there will transpire a complete turnaround of worldly values. Those who have elbowed and kicked their way to the top will find themselves thrown off the ladder, while those now on the bottom will ascend thrones to reign with Christ forever and ever. "Blessed are the meek, for they shall inherit the earth."

At present none of this is very obvious, granted. It still seems the aggressive have the advantage, that self-assertive go-getters will indeed go further and get more than anyone else.

But Jesus made a promise in this Beatitude, and we either believe him or we don't. One thing we can't deny, though: he believed it. He was content to live in meekness, to entrust himself to the ultimate victory of the God who had called him. And according to Scripture, that humility led Jesus into great blessedness: "He humbled himself and became obedient unto death, even death on a cross. Therefore God has highly exalted him and bestowed on him the name which is above every name, that at the name of Jesus every knee should bow, in heaven and on earth and under the earth, and every tongue confess that Jesus Christ is Lord, to the glory of God the Father" (Phil 2:8-11).

Study Questions

1. Is our society obsessed with winning? Please give some examples.
2. Cite both good and bad aspects of ambition.
3. What percentage of praise do you receive for achievements vs. sensitive qualities such as gentleness and kindness?
4. How do our insecurities push us to achieve?
5. Why do Christians have worth whether they win, lose or tie?
6. What are some specific ways in which you could practice gentleness?
7. Why does gentleness take great strength?
8. Why does the gentle person not have a need to manipulate or control others?

*B*lessed are
those who hunger and
thirst for righteousness,
for they shall be filled.

5

THE BLESSED LONGING

We hold these truths to be self-evident," the Declaration of Independence says, "that all men are created equal, that they are endowed by their Creator with certain unalienable Rights, that among these are Life, Liberty and the pursuit of Happiness." The pursuit of happiness is the drive behind so much of what we do: the use of our time, the relationships we build, the things we buy, the vacations we take.

In the Beatitudes we've already considered, Jesus makes some startling statements. He has declared blessed the poor in spirit, the mourners, and the meek, and by now something important should be coming into focus for us: happiness is given to those who aren't looking for it. The poor in spirit, aware of their sin, don't feel worthy of it; the mourners, nursing their wounds, are looking at the cause of their grief; the meek, seeing themselves in the light of God's grace, are too amazed by what they *do* have to worry much about what they don't have. Happiness, then, must be a by-product of something else.

With all respect to the Declaration of Independence, the pursuit of happiness never succeeds. It's like hunting for Bigfoot in the forests of the Northwest—the adventure can keep you going a long time, but in the end you'll have little to show for the search. This is because happiness results from seeking something else.

What to Look For

Jesus tells us what we should seek: "Blessed are those who hunger and thirst for righteousness" (Mt 5:6).

Righteousness. The word sounds so . . . religious, so puritanical. It has the atmosphere of a dark sanctuary, smelling of mildew and old incense; it conjures images of lips pursed with disapproval and fingers wagging in condemnation. But what does it really mean?

In biblical language righteousness has to do with right relationships. It refers first to God: to be righteous means to love God, to live in the freedom of grace and the discipline of obedience. And it refers to those around us: to be righteous means to love others, to work for their welfare and to defend their rights. Thus the word has both a heavenly and an earthly orientation, a spiritual and a social dimension. Jesus said, "You shall love the Lord your God with all your heart, and with all your soul, and with all your mind. This is the great and first commandment. And the second is like it, you shall love your neighbor as yourself. On these two commandments depend all the law and the prophets" (Mt 22:37-40). The righteous live by these two commandments. "Blessed are those who hunger and thirst for righteousness." The Greek in this verse is interesting. Usually the verbs "to hunger" and "to thirst" take objects which would literally be translated with the words "of the," as in "I hunger for *of the bread*," that is, for part of the bread. But this Beatitude breaks the rule. The grammar indicates hunger for the whole thing, as in "I hunger for bread," that is, the whole loaf. Blessed are those, Jesus said, who hunger and thirst not simply for part of righteousness but for the whole thing.

Intense Desire

We might have expected Jesus to declare happy the righteous; it would surely be blessed to be rightly related to God and one's neighbors. But that's not what he said. Jesus congratulated not those who have it but those who want it—those who want it in the most intense way.

Words must be understood in context. We say, "I'm so hungry!" and we mean we'd like another pastry to hold us over until lunchtime. Or we say, "I'm so thirsty!" and we mean we'd like another Coke—perhaps the second or third of the afternoon. But in Jesus' day hunger and thirst were serious realities. To hunger meant feeling the Grim Reaper's scythe pierce your stomach, and to thirst meant feeling his hand clutch at your throat. To the person who really hungers and thirsts, nothing else matters; all other desires become insignificant. Blessed is the person who longs for righteousness as though his or her life depended on it.

Now, I think most of us have already begun to hunger and thirst, though we may not know exactly what we want. What we do know is that unfulfillment gnaws at our insides; we desire something more out of life. So, with a nutritional ignorance about things of the spirit, we often seek relief by eating junk food. We try to satisfy our longings with new relationships, or larger houses and sportier cars, or with greater professional achievements, or zippier sex lives. These things are potato chips. Nothing wrong with potato chips—in their place. But you can't live on them. They might quiet the gurgling noises of hunger for a while, but they won't keep you alive in the long run. You need something more nutritious.

Diogenes Allen has described this inner hunger by drawing on an image from astronomy:

> There is an emptiness at our core that is like a Black Hole, a black hole in space. A Black Hole sucks down all matter, and there is an emptiness in us which threatens to suck us down as well, although what it is actually doing is dispelling an illusion. It is not destroying us, but revealing to us that we are already a dead thing trying to give itself life by taking all within its reach. But the core of us remains an emptiness. To be a person, a soul, is to need something beyond oneself to live; whatever we can *grasp* cannot give us life. No matter what efforts we make to fill ourselves, we always find ourselves once again empty.

The hunger within can reveal something important: we need more than we can grasp for ourselves. The first step in hungering and thirsting for righteousness, then, is hungering and thirsting, period. We must let ourselves feel the pain of the longing. Eating potato chips relieves the pangs only temporarily; eventually, the Black Hole of Hunger engulfs us with desire. The truth is, we need more than we realize, and thus we cannot allow ourselves to be satisfied by things within our reach.

Going Home

Only one food will satisfy: the righteousness of God. As Rudyard Kipling lay ill, he stirred. The attending nurse asked, "Do you want anything?" Kipling answered, "I want God!" Whether we realize it or not, this is what we all want; the reason for our inner discontent is that we long for a right relationship with God, for righteousness.

And blessed are those who know it. Congratulations to those who have faced the void and named the object of their desire, for they are closer to being satisfied than they realize. When the prodigal finds himself knee-deep in pig slop, with cramping stomach and convicting conscience, he decides to do something about it. He pushes through squealing pigs, stomps mud off his feet, and heads for his father's house.

When you're really hungry or thirsty, you're not satisfied simply to be aware of the fact. No, you do something. If you want food and drink, you go to a kitchen or restaurant. If you want professional advancement, you work harder and stay longer at the office. If you want a good family life, you schedule time with your spouse and children. If you want to learn, you get a good book and study.

The rules don't suddenly change when it comes to the spiritual life! If you want—*really* want—righteousness, you will do certain things. What does someone do who hungers and thirsts for righteousness? The answer varies in details from person to person, of course, but a general pattern can be described.

Loving God

Those who hunger and thirst for righteousness want to love God more fully. They know that though they don't have a spiritual dime to their name (poor in spirit), though they've spilt plenty of milk to cry over (mourners), though they really aren't much to brag about (meek), they have been claimed by an amazing Grace that will not let them go. And in this joyous freedom they gratefully offer themselves to God. They know they can never become good enough to deserve such perfect, aggressive love; they can never, on their own, achieve such mercy. But for that very reason they want to please God. They want to be the kind of people who make God smile in approval. Like children, loved and cared for and therefore secure, they want to make their Father proud.

So, to put it negatively, those who hunger and thirst for righteousness refrain from doing certain things; they avoid anything that comes between God and them.

Some things take the edge off our spiritual lives. They may not be particularly evil in themselves; they probably didn't make it into the Top Ten on Moses' tablets. But they undercut—often subtlety, almost imperceptibly—our relationship with God. An R-rated movie, perhaps, or a trashy book, or too much television, or conversations with certain people, or mental fantasies, or a party scene, or a good thing given an unbalanced prominence—almost anything can come between God and us. Most of us know our vulnerabilities, the things that make us feel spiritually out of sorts. If we desire righteousness, we will avoid these things as we avoid germs or carcinogens.

To put it positively, those who hunger and thirst do things that enhance their relationships with God. Hunger and thirst lead to action.

When you're hungry, feeling rumbles of discontent in your stomach, you do something about it: you go to the kitchen, prowl about the cupboards and refrigerator, and get something to eat. Or you go to a restaurant, survey the options, and order a meal.

In the same way, hunger and thirst for righteousness draws us to places where we're likely to find spiritual food and drink. For many centuries God's people have identified certain places wherein they encounter the presence of God, wherein they feel lifted by grace and challenged to obedience.

Where are these places? God meets and renews us through the Word, through studying Scripture and hearing the preaching of the Church. God meets and renews us in worship with the people of Jesus Christ. God meets and renews us in community with our sisters and brothers in faith. God meets and renews us in the needs of the poor and oppressed. Those who want a right relationship with God will head for these places like prodigals going home, and they will meet a waiting, welcoming Father.

A woman once told me about a change she had recently experienced. Her college years were marred by a lifestyle she now regrets—drugs, parties, not much studying. But she married a good man, a man who loved her and provided all the material comforts she could want.

"I'm very well-off," she said. I noticed her jewelry and knew she wasn't kidding. "But I wasn't happy. I felt such a hunger for . . . something, I wasn't sure what. I just knew there had to be more to life.

"One day I happened to drive by your church, and I wondered whether this might be where I would find whatever I was looking for. So I came the next Sunday. Not knowing what to expect, I was a little afraid.

"But something happened in that worship service. I felt the presence of God, and I sensed God speaking to me through your sermon. I knew I had come to the right place."

Loving Our Neighbors

Those who hunger and thirst for righteousness also want to love those around them more fully. They avoid things that come between them and others, and they do things that enhance their relationship with others.

Certain attitudes, like termites, eat at a relationship until only a hollowed-out, wobbly structure remains standing. When we envy another's recognition, for example, or covet another's possession, we allow something evil to chew its way between us and our neighbors. And certain deeds knock the structure over altogether. When we speak words only loosely held together by cords of truth, say, or when we manipulate others to our advantage, we kick the relationship into the dust. Those who hunger and thirst for righteousness avoid these things.

And they do the things that enhance their relationships. Like the Samaritan Jesus called good, they let themselves be troubled by the needs of others: they make time, they listen, they take on problems, they do what they can to help.

The Choices We Make

Hungering and thirsting for righteousness is about making choices. We have an inner longing for something more, most of us do, and we must pay attention to that desire, let its pain bite into our souls, try to understand it. When we realize that what we really want is righteousness—a right relationship with God and others—we then face choices in the use of our time and energies.

It's hard to know what to say about someone who says, "Yes, I'd really like a better relationship with God, and I'd like to love people more," but then doesn't do anything to make these things happen. If a man announced he was starving but didn't look for food, you'd have to doubt either his sanity or truthfulness; if a woman said she was dying of thirst but did nothing to find drink, you'd wonder where she lost her marbles or why she was lying.

Let's admit it: the things we really desire, we work to get. God isn't fooled, and we might as well quit trying to fool ourselves. God has set before us an awesome amount of freedom, and how we use it not only proves our deepest values but also does something to us, changes us. C. S. Lewis wrote: "Every time you make a choice you are turning that central part of you, the part that chooses, into something a little different from what it was before. And taking your life as a whole, with all your innumerable choices, you are slowly turning this central thing either into a heavenly creature or into a hellish creature and either into a creature that is in harmony with God or else into one that is in a state of war with God."

Satisfaction Guaranteed

Blessed are those who make the right choices, who organize days and use talents and invest energies and spend money and burn passions on things that lead to greater righteousness. Congratulations to them, Jesus said, "for they shall be satisfied."

This, then, is why those who hunger and thirst for righteousness will be happy: their hunger will be filled and their thirst assuaged. They will be given righteousness.

They will be *given* righteousness. We want and look for it, but in truth it can't be found; it can only be received. We hunger and thirst for it, but can only position ourselves to receive it. Righteousness always comes as a gift. But be certain of this: it does come. The desires of all who want a right relationship with God and others will be satisfied. This is the gospel truth through Jesus Christ the Reconciler, the promise of God, a gift to be accepted with childlike trust.

Study Questions

1. How would you describe righteousness?
2. What does the author mean when he states that righteousness has both a spiritual and social dimension?
3. Describe a person who hungers and thirsts for righteousness.
4. What are the good aspects of hunger and thirst?
5. How will you choose to use your time and energy if what you really want is righteousness?
6. What is God's promise to those who hunger and thirst for righteousness?
7. What does the author mean when he states that righteousness is a gift?

Blessed
are the merciful,
for they shall
obtain mercy.

6

THE GIFT
OF MERCY

T he first four Beatitudes declare happiness for the needy—
spiritual beggars, mourners, the meek and those who hunger
and thirst for righteousness. Jesus congratulated people with
these attitudes because God is on their side. God turns with mercy
toward those who have nothing else—and *know* they have nothing
else—on which to rely. Thus they are blessed . . . happy.

In the fifth blessing those who have received mercy are shown
they must give it away. "Blessed are the merciful, for they shall
obtain mercy" (Mt 5:7).

Given Away or Lost
Some things must be given away or they'll be lost, must be offered

with open hands or they'll slip through clenched fingers.

From grade school through college I played the trumpet and was, frankly, pretty good. I happily shared my gift with all who would listen, from practice sessions which insulted the ears of long-suffering parents to musical competitions which won favor from critical judges. But one day I stopped playing; my gift became a private possession I thought I could keep to myself. And hot lips turned into flabby lips; a young man who had been able to blow Bach couldn't do much more than blow up a balloon.

If you hoard certain gifts, you lose them. Mercy is such a gift. God freely offers it to us; we cannot earn it; we do not deserve it. It's ours for the taking. But we *must* pass it on. Mercy stored up is like fruit kept too long: it spoils, goes sour. Unless we offer to others the mercy we ourselves have received, we will be judged without mercy.

What does it mean to be merciful?

Reactive Mercy

The stresses of sharing life with other human beings inevitably lead to pain. We all get wounded at one time or another by gossip, jealousies, betrayals, broken promises, insensitivities. Some wounds merely scratch the skin, needing not much more than a Band-Aid, but others penetrate the heart, needing intensive care for the spirit.

The people who will be most happy, Jesus said, are those who respond to such wounds with mercy, who overlook minor offenses and forgive major ones. Blessed are those who respond with mercy.

Well, all right. But it's not easy, is it? Sometimes it seems easier to ignore an approaching hurricane than to disregard pain that others have blown into our lives.

Why is it so difficult to be merciful? It has to do with wanting to protect ourselves. If you've wounded me I will instinctively build a fortress to prevent more arrows from penetrating. I will assert myself—insist on my rights, protect my dignity, demand my space—against you. I've heard enough sermons to know I should forgive. But that would leave me open to further attack; I would feel weak, vulnerable. So fear takes command of the situation and marshals my inner resources for defense.

The problem is this: garrisons of self-protection separate and isolate. So while I might be able to defend myself in the short run, I will destroy myself in the long run, for I cannot live without community.

And neither can you. We were created to need relationships—with other humans and with God. The only way to survive, then, to be happy, is to risk the vulnerability of forgiveness, to hang on to the cord of fellowship no matter how cut and frayed it may be.

Jacinta Diaz was not an outspoken leader in her Puerto Rican church; she held no office, no position of authority. But she was known as a woman of great faith. The villagers thought of her as the one whose prayers God would most likely answer.

One night her son was relaxing in a bar about a half mile from town and got into an argument that turned nasty. Angry words turned to threats. Threats turned to fighting. Within a few minutes he lay dead on the floor.

Word of the tragedy spread quickly through the small town. Soon Jacinta and a few friends were together in her home pouring out their anguished grief.

The bar was in turmoil. Remorse overwhelmed the young man who had killed her son. He cried, "What have I done, what have I done?" He talked of taking his own life. In utter despair he said, "Please, please bring Jacinta." He did not realize it was her son whom he had killed.

The young man's pleas reached Jacinta's house. A neighbor said, "He must be crazy! He wants you to comfort him!" But Jacinta, rising from her grief, walked down the half mile of country road to the bar. She spoke quietly, and putting healing hands on her son's killer, prayed with him.

Jacinta Diaz, blessed Jacinta Diaz, holding together by mercy the unraveling cord of community, showed herself a child of God. For God hangs on, too, though sin has done its damnedest to cut us free. God holds together the relationship by accepting the abuse, suffering the shame. God dresses down into the vulnerability of frail humanity, and the thorns and nails and spear, piercing more than flesh, sink into a holy, grieving heart. And then, no cries of anger, no vows of revenge, no protective defenses. Only a prayer: "Father, forgive them; for they know not what they do" (Lk 23:34).

Blessed are those who respond with Godlike mercy to the aggravations and aggressions coming their way. Though wounded like their Lord, they will be far happier than those who protect themselves against the unjust Golgothas of life.

Searching Mercy

The mercy Jesus declared blessed must be defined by Jesus himself. Our own notions are too cramped by fallible minds and self-centered hearts. Only by staying attentive to Jesus—his life, death and resurrection—can we properly understand this Beatitude, for he concretely embodied the mercy of God.

In Jesus we see an aggressive side to mercy. Through him God took the initiative. God didn't wait for us to mend the broken relationship. Like the waiting father who *ran* to meet his prodigal son, God sped down the corridors of eternity and hurdled the barricades of our sin to embrace us in love. God entered our world, took responsibility for saving us from the mess we had gotten our-selves into and found us before we even knew we were lost. God-like mercy, the mercy Jesus revealed in his life and congratulated in the fifth Beatitude, is impatient . . . assertive.

This active, searching mercy has at least four characteristics: it sees, understands, helps and advocates.

The Eyes of Mercy

The merciful don't wait for problems to come their way. They look for trouble; they search the horizon of human experience to find people in need.

Make no mistake about it, we see what we want to see. The abundance and variety of life force us to be selective in our percep-tions. We can't take it all in, and so inevitably we decide to notice some things and not others.

What someone chooses to see, furthermore, says much about his or her character. One person looks at a bag lady picking through garbage and sees a child of God caught in the hopeless snare of poverty; another person looks at the same bag lady and sees a lazy bum who won't get off her duff to find a job. One person looks at a welfare program and sees an attempt to provide justice and equal-ity for all; another person looks at the same program and sees nothing but a meddling, over-taxing government that's gotten too big for its political britches. We tend to see things according to our values and prejudices and comforts, and what we see, in turn, confirms those same values and prejudices and comforts.

In January 1988 Karen Toshima, a twenty-seven-year-old graphic artist, was caught in the crossfire of rival drug gangs and died on the sidewalk in front of a fashionable restaurant in west side Los Angeles. The city's establishment reacted with horror. The story was headlined by newspapers and television for days. Thirty police officers were assigned the case, and a city councilman offered a $25,000 reward for information.

Ten days later, Alma Lee Washington was sitting in her wheelchair in the doorway of her run-down two-bedroom house in south central Los Angeles. Hoodlums drove by and opened fire with a .45 caliber handgun. The sixty-seven-year-old black woman was killed when a bullet struck her right eye. But almost no one noticed. The newspapers barely mentioned the incident, and just two officers were assigned the case.

The city chose to see the murder of a young woman in an affluent neighborhood; the city chose to ignore the murder of an old woman in a poor neighborhood.

What we choose to see makes a difference. The merciful keep their eyes open; they want to see things that others miss; they search the dark corners of life, looking for trouble in which to show the love of God.

As I think of my own selective perception, I know I would rather keep certain mental pictures in the back of my memory. But they're elbowing their way forward. I've recently been to Africa, visiting mission hospitals, roaming through villages and preaching. I'm not yet able to subdue with words the emotional storm within me; so many impressions, so many thoughts. It will take time to sort it out. As part of that process, I will have to decide which images to remember. Some I would prefer not to see again: distended-bellied children, now dead; empty eyes with nothing in view but more suffering; mothers trying to nurse little skeletons back to life with dried, shriveled breasts. A part of me would prefer not to see again these things, for they disturb my comfort and trouble my peace, and much in my active life will conspire to crowd them out of my consciousness.

But then I hear Jesus say, "Blessed are the merciful, for they shall obtain mercy," and I have set before me the possibility of blessed-ness—happiness!—if only I keep watch over this dark shadow. That's what the merciful do: they stay at their posts, searching the horizon long after the sun has set and others have gone into the comfort of the camp. The merciful see the three million homeless and keep watching. The merciful see the forty thousand who die of starvation each day and keep watching. The merciful see the undocumented aliens in their makeshift huts and keep watching. The merciful see the lonely old man down the street who smells like a cheap nursing home and showers with spittle when he talks, and they keep watching. They keep watching. The merciful see.

The Heart of Mercy

After seeing a problem, the merciful try to understand it. It's not enough simply to notice a need; something must be done about it. Before action can be taken, however, something must be *known* about it.

Understanding requires *listening*. This is difficult, very difficult. It's so much easier to make judgments based on what we think we already know, so much easier, especially, to jump to conclusions absolving us of responsibility. If the homeless would get jobs and quit lying around. . . . If the undocumented would have stayed in Mexico. . . . If he hadn't been so promiscuous. . . . If she had thought about that before filing for divorce . . . and so on. Things can seem pretty clear when you're comfortably removed from a problem. But the merciful stifle the inner voices of prejudice long enough to learn, to hear the hurts, to see the larger picture.

Calvin Coolidge, during the first days of his presidency, con-tinued to reside with his family in their third-floor suite at the

Willard Hotel in Washington. Early one morning he awoke to see a cat burglar going through his clothes, removing a wallet and a watch chain.

Coolidge said, "I wish you wouldn't take that . . . I don't mean the watch and chain, only the charm. Read what is engraved on the back of it." The burglar read, "Presented to Calvin Coolidge, Speaker of the House, by the Massachusetts General Court."

The president identified himself and persuaded the startled thief to relinquish the watch charm. Then Coolidge instead of calling Secret Service agents, engaged him in quiet conversation. He learned that the young man and his college roommate were unable to pay their hotel bill and buy train tickets back to their campus. So he counted out thirty-two dollars from his wallet, declared it a loan, and advised the student to leave, in order to avoid detection, as unconventionally as he had entered.

Coolidge listened, which led to understanding, which led to mercy.

And understanding also requires *identification*. By identification I mean what Father Zosima in *The Brothers Karamazov* said of compassion—that it involves humility, and humility consists "not in lying down, but in standing up, one by one, in the other's shoes." The merciful put themselves in the other's position; they let themselves feel the hurt and bear the shame. They freely take on a problem as if it were their own.

So when the bishop called for a volunteer to go to Molokai and remain for life amidst the lepers (with the certainty of the volunteer becoming a leper himself), Father Damien sprang to his feet and pleaded to be allowed to live and work—and die—among the lepers.

And when Kagawa, as a student, became aware of the suffering in the slums around his seminary, he left the comfort of his dormitory room and moved into a six-by-six room he shared with the drunks and derelicts of Kobe, Japan.

And when Dave Allen had persuaded Robbie—a paraplegic confined to a wheelchair—to attend summer camp, he got himself a wheelchair, and for the entire week kept himself in it so Robbie wouldn't be alone, so Robbie would have at least one friend who knew firsthand the struggle of a toilet stall and the strain of a rocky trail and the pain of watching other kids play volleyball.

Mercy grows out of understanding, and understanding comes from listening and identifying.

The Hands of Mercy

After seeing a problem and trying to understand it, the merciful do what they can to help. When I'm sick I want more than a doctor who understands my problem; I want the proper treatment that will bring healing. Understanding must lead to action, must be converted into the currency of concrete assistance.

Jesus told about a Samaritan who was good because he did what he could. The traveler interrupted his journey, bathed the victim's wounds with oil, put him on a donkey, took him to the inn where he was known and promised to reimburse the innkeeper the cost of nursing him back to life. He was a merciful man, this Samaritan.

Not everyone who stumbles over a need is that helpful. A few years ago two researchers conducted an experiment with forty Princeton Seminary students. Each seminarian was instructed to walk to a nearby building and dictate an impromptu talk into a tape recorder. Some were told to talk on the Good Samaritan parable, others on their career concerns. Unknown to the students, the researchers had planted an actor along the pathway who, as a student approached, groaned and slumped to the ground.

Human Behavior magazine reported on the experiment: sixty per cent walked right by, and some who were planning their talk on the Good Samaritan literally stepped over the slumped body. There was no significant difference between those who had the parable on their minds and those who were thinking about future careers.

The aspiring ministers were probably no worse than other goal-oriented people busy with their affairs. In this Beatitude, though, Jesus tells us that if we will stop our frantic pursuit of elusive happiness long enough to help broken people along the way, we will, in fact, find authentic happiness. *"Blessed* are the merciful . . ."

Following World War 2, German students volunteered to help rebuild an English cathedral, a casualty of the Luftwaffe bombings. As work progressed a debate broke out on how best to restore a large statue of Christ with outstretched arms bearing the inscription, "Come unto me." Careful patching could repair all the damage, except for the hands which had been destroyed by bomb fragments. Should they attempt the delicate reconstruction of those hands?

The workers reached a decision that stands today. The statue has no hands, and the inscription reads, "Christ has no hands but ours."

The hands of mercy are the hands of Christ.

The Voice of Mercy

Mercy has eyes that see, a heart that understands, hands that help and, finally, a voice that speaks. Mercy won't keep quiet. It pleads for the powerless, defends the defenseless, sounds off for the silent.

The merciful are not pushovers; in fact, they can be quite pushy. Florence Nightingale became a heroine of Victorian England as she nursed soldiers of the Crimean War. What is not as well known about her is that she made her greatest contribution working for better hospital conditions and improved nursing care. As often happens with advocates, she provoked hostility from doctors and the military establishment, but she persisted, and because of her aggressive mercy thousands of lives were saved.

The merciful are like Abraham praying that Sodom would be spared. The merciful are like Moses pleading with God to forgive Israel's idolatry, "and if not," he said, "blot me, I pray thee, out of thy book which thou hast written" (Ex 32:32). The merciful are like David demanding respect for the king who was trying to murder him. The merciful are like Jeremiah and Micah and Amos defending the rights of the poor. The merciful are like Jesus weeping over Jerusalem, like Jesus who, according to the Apostle, sits at the right hand of God the Father interceding for us. Blessed are those who join with these in raising their voices on behalf of others.

The Unbroken Circle

"Blessed are the merciful . . ." Happy will be those who look for trouble, understand it, do what they can to help, and become advocates for those hurt by it. They are to be congratulated.

Why? "For they shall obtain mercy."

Mercy moves in a circle. Having received mercy, we give it away, and we receive even more. Mercy multiplies.

Louis B. Mayer, founder of Metro-Goldwyn-Mayer, once told about a fight he had in childhood. He assured his mother that the other boy was entirely at fault. She said nothing, but after washing his black eyes, took him to the back door of their home. Nearby stood several hills that created a fine echo. She told Louis to call those hills all the bad names he could think of. He did so, and all the names came back to him. "Now," she said, "call out, 'God bless you.' " He did so, and back came, "God bless you." Mayer said he never forgot that lesson. What you give to others you get back from them.

Dr. Paul Brand, in *In His Image*, tells of his mother, a remarkable woman who served for many years as a medical missionary in India. She was a merciful woman who had the blessings of mercy echoed back to her.

At the age of seventy-five while working in the mountains of South India, she fell and broke her hip. Not until the next morning did a workman find her lying on the floor in pain. Four men carried her on a makeshift cot down the mountain and put her in a jeep for a 150-mile pounding over rutted roads.

Dr. Brand soon visited his mother's mud-walled home to persuade her to retire. She could barely walk, needing two bamboo canes for balance as she painfully pulled her paralyzed feet behind her. Yet she continued to travel on horseback and camp in the villages; she preached the gospel, treated sicknesses and pulled decayed teeth.

There were certainly good reasons for her retirement, but Granny Brand threw them off like so much nonsense. Who would continue the ministry? "In any case," she concluded the matter, "what is the use of preserving my old body if it is not going to be used where God needs me?"

So she stayed. She didn't stop riding her pony until she was ninety-three, and then only because she kept falling off. But even then she managed. Devoted Indians carried her on a hammock from town to town until she finally died at the age of ninety-five.

Dr. Brand remembers seeing his mother in a village in the mountains, one of his last visual memories of her:

She was sitting on a low stone wall that circles the village, with people pressing in from all sides. They are listening to all she has to say about Jesus. Heads are nodding in encouragement, and deep, searching questions come from the crowd. Granny's own rheumy eyes are shining, and standing beside her I can see what she must be seeing through failing eyes: intent faces gazing with absolute trust and affection on the one they have grown to love.

I know that even with my relative youth and strength and all my specialized knowledge about health and agricultural techniques, I could never command that kind of devotion and love from these people. They are looking at a wrinkled old face, but somehow her shrunken tissues have become transparent and she is all lambent spirit. To them, she is beautiful.

Mercy moves in a circle: having received the gift, we give it away, and we receive it back again—from others and from God. It's like a great game in which players pass on a ball as soon as it's caught; so long as the ball keeps moving, the sport continues and with it the joy.

But if the ball stops, the game stops. Woe to the person who breaks the circle! The Bible warns that the unmerciful shall not obtain mercy.

This sobering corollary to the fifth Beatitude shouldn't be ignored. If you keep mercy to yourself, you won't receive it from others; worse, you won't receive it from God. Well, how could you? You would have broken the circle. In hoarding the ball, you wouldn't know the joy of catching it, of playing the game.

So, happy are those who keep the ball moving. "Blessed are the merciful, for they shall obtain mercy."

Study Questions

1. Can you give an example of a gift you hoarded only to lose it?
2. What does it mean to be merciful? Have you experienced it?
3. Why is it so difficult to be merciful?
4. What did Jesus do when he saw injustice and inequality? What should we do?
5. What are some steps the merciful might take after they have noticed a need?
6. Explain the circle of mercy and then try to test it out in your life to see how it works.
7. What will happen to the person who breaks the circle of mercy?

*B*lessed are
the pure in heart,
for they shall
see God.

CHAPTER

7

CLEAR AT
THE CENTER

What would we do without the language of the heart? We speak of heartfelt desire and heartless actions, of heartaches and heartstrings, of passionate hearts and true hearts, of broken hearts and bleeding hearts, of the heart of the matter and the heart of the city. And none of this has anything to do with the organ that pumps blood through bodies; it has to do with the center of things.

When Robert Pirsig, in *Zen and the Art of Motorcycle Maintenance,* writes that "the place to improve the world is first in one's own heart . . . and then work outward from there," he is saying that we must begin at the center of our own lives.

The modern use of the word hasn't changed much from the days of the Bible. In Hebrew psychology the heart was the human center, the seat of personal feeling, willing and thinking.

Pure at the Center

"Blessed are the pure in heart" (Mt 5:8), Jesus said. Happy are those who are pure at the center of their lives. Whoa! At this point in Jesus' sermon we might cringe in guilt and fear. This sounds considerably more difficult than the other Beatitudes. Perhaps we could identify with the poor in spirit, the mourners, the meek, and those who hunger and thirst for righteousness; perhaps we could even imagine ourselves becoming more merciful because of the mercy we ourselves have received. But pure in heart? If happiness depends on purity of heart, we might think, we're up a raging river without a paddle; we might as well get used to being tossed about by the white-water turbulence of unhappiness.

But let's try to understand what Jesus said before giving up. What does it mean to be *pure* in heart? The basic meaning of the Greek word is unmixed, unadulterated, unalloyed. We use the word in a similar way in English when we speak of "pure gold" or "pure maple syrup."

Purity of heart, therefore, has to do with singularity of purpose. The pure in heart are not double-minded, unstable in all their ways (Jas 1:7); they don't waffle and waver in their convictions. Søren Kierkegaard wrote a remarkable book titled, *Purity of Heart Is to Will One Thing.* That's a good way to state it.

Mixed Motives

But how often do we have singular motives? Even the best we do is tainted with motives that are, if not evil, nothing we'd like paraded before the world. I am writing this book for the good reason of wanting to help people find authentic happiness by following the teaching of Jesus. But there are other reasons, too: I want the satisfaction of using my gifts and being productive; I want—this hurts to admit—to be liked and respected; I want—this *really* hurts to admit—the royalties on the sale of the book. Now, I'm not proud of these motives and God knows I regularly ask to be delivered from them, but they're part of the truth of who I am. And I suppose I take some consolation in believing I'm not alone; there are few things that even the best of us do with complete purity of intention.

Perhaps one reason singleness of purpose is harder to find than clean air in Los Angeles is our fear of commitment. To devote ourselves to one thing means excluding other things. This can be difficult.

A columnist for the *San Diego Union* told of a debate that took place 130 years ago on the floor of the U. S. Senate. The issue was whether the sale of liquor should be legal in certain territories that were seeking statehood. One notoriously anti-alcohol senator—who, according to one description, "was so dry, he was a known fire hazard"—challenged a colleague to stand and state his position. The uncommitted senator supposedly rose and replied as follows:

You've asked me how I feel about whiskey. Well, here's how I stand on the question.

If when you say whiskey, you mean that devil's brew, the poison spirit, the bloody monster that defiles innocence, dethrones reason, destroys the home and creates misery and poverty—yes, literally takes bread from the mouths of little children; if you mean the evil drink that topples the Christian man from the pinnacle of righteousness and gracious living and causes him to descend to the pit of degradation, despair, shame and helplessness, then I am certainly against it with all my heart.

But if when you say whiskey, you mean the oil of conversation, the philosophic wine, the ale consumed when good fellows get together, that puts a song in their heart and laughter on their lips, the warm glow of contentment in their eyes; if you mean Christmas cheer; if you mean the stimulating drink that puts the spring in an old man's footsteps on a frosty morning; if you mean the drink whose sale puts untold millions of dollars into our Treasury which are used to provide tender care for our little crippled children, our blind or deaf or dumb, our pitifully aged and infirm, to build highways and hospitals and schools, then I am certainly in favor of it.

This is my stand, and I will not compromise.

The senator must have been running for re-election. But we're all familiar with the difficulty of achieving singleness of mind. It's tough to be committed; we'd rather keep our options open.

Most of us, I'm convinced, want to live well, to do what is right. Unfortunately we want other things, too. Temptation threatens when it gets us imagining other possibilities. We know, for example, that God wants sexual purity for us, sex kept within the loving framework of marriage. But we don't have to be students of *Playboy* or *Playgirl* to picture ourselves in different situations. And if our imaginations start to wander, our bodies may not be far behind. This dividedness of mind, then, becomes sin's first foothold in this area of our lives.

Uniting a Divided Heart

How do you achieve singleness of purpose? First, I can tell you what not to do: don't try to tell yourself to stop thinking of something. You won't be able to think of anything else. David Seamands tells the story of the alchemist who sold villagers a powder he claimed would turn water into gold. "But when you mix it," he said, "you must never think of red monkeys, or it won't work." No one ever got the gold, of course, because you can't force yourself not to think of something.

No, you won't achieve singleness of purpose by trying to chase distracting things out of your mind. How do you find purity of heart? *You must focus your attention on something big enough to unite a divided heart.*

There is something—someone, really—big enough to unify our hearts and therefore purify us. Jesus doesn't mock us; he doesn't bless the pure in heart, and then wink at us, as if he knows no one will ever really achieve it; he doesn't do what he accused the Pharisees of doing—lay heavy burdens and not lift a finger to help. He takes us seriously in these Beatitudes, and we must take him seriously. If he congratulated the pure in heart, purity of heart is a genuine possibility.

This Beatitude of Jesus, as with all his teaching, must be understood as part of the gospel, as *good* news. Jesus truthfully expressed the will of God, and this alone makes him worth hearing. But there's more to it: Jesus not only taught the will of God; he lived it.

If being pure in heart seems impossible for us, we must remember that Jesus has achieved it in our place. He perfectly obeyed the law of God; he gave himself wholeheartedly, without mixture of motives, to God's will. Jesus was *the* pure-in-heart one.

Thus purity of heart becomes a genuine possibility for us *in him.* God's grace is this: when we entrust our lives to Jesus Christ, his life becomes our life, his obedience our obedience, his purity our purity. The only thing left for us is to look to him.

Captivated by Christ

The pure in heart look to Jesus Christ; he is the object of their single-mindedness. They don't turn their eyes upon their own purity or lack of purity; they don't notice themselves at all. They look only to Jesus Christ. This is why Dietrich Bonhoeffer said, "The pure in heart have a child-like simplicity like Adam before the fall, innocent alike of good and evil."

There are well-meaning Christians who need the liberation of purity of heart. They want to please God, and so they monitor their every step (forward or backward) in such things as prayer and Bible study; they relentlessly, mercilessly examine themselves. No scientist every watched a lab experiment more carefully. They appear to be mature believers, serious disciples. We may admire them.

But we should pity them. Spiritual navel gazing is as sinful as any other self-centeredness, even though it's covered with a veneer of piety. And such self-preoccupation always leads to restlessness and guilt. No one ever gets spiritual enough to feel at peace with himself or herself.

Congratulations to the pure in heart! They have been released from themselves and enjoy the freedom of being captivated by Jesus Christ. Their own spirituality or lack of it isn't half so interesting as their Lord. So they are content to see only him.

And in seeing Jesus Christ, the pure in heart see God. This is why they are so blessed, why they should be congratulated. In the language of John's Gospel, those who have seen the Son have seen the Father.

Seeing God

By looking wholly to Jesus Christ, the pure in heart see God; their singular focus enables them to know the divine character and purposes. You can't see anything very well if you're looking in two directions at once. In personal relationships, for example, dating a variety of people won't allow you to know anyone very deeply. You must eventually limit yourself to one person, and from that singular focus emerges a fuller knowledge. As the self-limiting narrows into marriage, you learn more and more, until you *know* the person who shares your bed and couch and table.

The pure in heart will know God because they have narrowed their focus to Jesus Christ; they are not distracted by their own spirituality, or their own ideas about what God ought to be like, or anything else.

And the pure in heart keep looking at God through Jesus Christ. This, too, is why they see God. For we see most clearly those things toward which we keep our attention riveted. Isn't this the point of all sustained study? As you open yourself to something it reveals its deepest secrets. I can look up at the night sky and see a billion pinpoints of light, and if I pause to think about it, can be over-whelmed by the grandeur of the universe. But an astronomer sees so much more; because she has looked and not stopped looking at the night sky, she is able to see planets and constellations and galaxies and things I don't even know how to name.

The last time I visited the National Gallery in London, I planned to do something different from the usual high-speed tourist sweep. I determined to look very carefully at just a few paintings. So I placed myself in front of Rembrandt's re-creation of a famous biblical scene—the woman caught in adultery. I had seen it before, but this time I wanted to see deeper into it, let it do something to me.

Staying in one place was harder than I expected. My compulsive, achievement-oriented personality wanted to visit all the rooms and see all the paintings. But I forced myself to keep looking at Rem-brandt's masterpiece. Other visitors came and went; I tried not to notice them. The painting was what I wanted to see, simply the painting. And indeed I began to see things I had never seen before; like the gospel itself, it had layers and layers of meaning waiting to be discovered.

One woman helped me keep watch. As others passed by, she stayed. We did not move, two embedded rocks in a swift stream of humanity. I thought I saw, out of the corner of my eye, a tear step down her cheeks. Was she identifying with the woman in the painting? Or the arrogant Pharisees? One thing for sure: the Lord was touching her, too. And together we stood there, aware of each other but focused on the painting, a community of faith, silent as Quakers before the mystery of grace. What it did for her, I can't say; we never spoke. But I was changed. I saw things I hadn't seen before, in the painting, in the gospel, in me.

The pure in heart look to God revealed in Jesus Christ, and keep on looking. For this reason, they shall see God. When? Today and tomorrow. The promise of this Beatitude has both a present and future aspect to it.

The Present and Future God

The pure in heart see God in the present. They've opened their eyes to God's self-revelation in Christ, and where others see only ordinary history, the pure in heart see the activity of God; where others see only pain, the pure in heart see the testing of God; where others see only the mechanics and mysteries of creation, the pure in heart see the creativity of God; where others see only a faltering religious institution, the pure in heart see the people of God; where others see only human speech-making, the pure in heart see the proclaimed Word of God; where others see only bread and wine, the pure in heart see the presence of God; where others see only natural recovery from illness, the pure in heart see the healing of God;

where others see only the vicissitudes of human love, the pure in heart see behind all human love the faithful love of God.

"The kingdom of God," Jesus said, "is in the midst of you" (Lk 17:21). The pure in heart see the hand of the reigning God in the present.

And they will see God in the future. They look forward to the fulfillment of their prayer, "Thy kingdom come" (Mt 6:10). The New Testament writings, like discordant music awaiting resolution in a dominant chord, have an incompleteness about them; they were written with expectancy, with eager longing for the return of Christ. The authors of the Gospels and Epistles, though individually unique in other ways, were agreed that their Lord would consummate all that he started in his earthly life and ministry.

And when this reign of God through him becomes fully manifest, the pure in heart will see God with a clarity not possible in this life. "Now we see in a mirror dimly," the apostle said, "but then face to face" (1 Cor 13:12). The veil will be pulled back. All that now obscures the vision will be removed, and those who have kept their eyes on Jesus Christ will behold the glory of God.

Getting Ready

Scripture promises, to those who look to Jesus Christ, an eternal audience with the King of kings. This expectation ought to gather together scattered thoughts and rivet attention on the Lord himself.

A chapter of my Ph.D. thesis was devoted to the theology of Jürgen Moltmann. Just as I started working on it, I discovered he was scheduled to lecture at the University of Edinburgh. A perfect opportunity, I thought, to hear his response to my ideas. I didn't know whether I would be able to meet him inasmuch as his visit would be brief, but I wanted to be prepared just in case.

For the next several weeks I lived with one thought—Jürgen Molt-mann. I read his books and articles; I thought about his theology by day and dreamt about it by night; I fantasized about the hoped-for encounter while jogging. I was single-minded about Jürgen Molt-mann, pure in heart when it came to him.

I was ready. At the conclusion of his presentation I followed him out into a winter night. Enough rain was falling to make you want to hail an ark instead of a taxi, and an angry wind was blowing as only it can off the Firth of Forth—an atmosphere hardly conducive to theological discussion, but my heart was set on it. So I grabbed the back of his arm and said, "Professor, may I speak with you a moment?"

He graciously invited me under his umbrella, and a conversation began that I will never forget. We stood, the two of us, oblivious to the inhospitable night, talking and debating the passion of our lives. It was far more than I had dared to hope for. And the dialog wouldn't have been possible had I not prepared myself for it.

If we take seriously the promise of Scripture that we are scheduled to meet the King of kings, we will want to get ourselves ready. Other things will lose their power to distract; the upcoming encounter, as a magnet, will draw all thoughts unto itself.

So the pure in heart are promised a vision of God, and the reverse, too, is true: the promised vision of God purifies the heart.

Not every chapel service I sat through during my year at Wheaton College was memorable; more than a few were endured only with an open *Time* magazine on my lap. But one will remain in my memory. The speaker was Dr. V. Raymond Edman, beloved past President of the College. His health had been precarious, and thus it was a special moment when he stepped to the pulpit.

His theme that morning was the need for reverence before God.

To illustrate his point he told of visiting Haile Selassie, then Emperor of Ethiopia. He described the preliminary briefings, the protocol he had to learn, and the way he bowed with respect as he entered the presence of the king. In the same way, he said, we must prepare ourselves to meet God.

At that moment, Dr. Edman slumped onto the pulpit, fell to the floor . . . and entered the presence of the King. God had granted him the one desire of his heart.

The pure in heart prepare themselves for the fulfillment of their one desire; knowing they shall one day enter the presence of the King of kings focuses their thoughts and disciplines their lives.

Do you see how this Beatitude has a circular movement to it? The pure in heart look to Jesus Christ, and seeing him, they see God—in the present and in the future—and knowing this keeps them even more focused on Jesus Christ who reveals God, and so on . . . and on . . . until they behold the glory of God.

Study Questions

1. What does it mean to be pure in heart?
2. Why is singleness of purpose so hard to find? *Not being able to focus on one thing → Jesus*
3. How do you achieve singleness of purpose?
4. Why should the pure of heart be congratulated?
5. What advice would you give someone who desires to see God more clearly?
6. What one thing can you do this week in your attempt to become pure of heart?

*B*lessed are
the peacemakers,
for they shall be called
sons of God.

CHAPTER

8

WAGING PEACE

One night during the Middle Ages, two warriors happened upon each other at a particularly dark spot in the road. The startled knights misinterpreted each other's movements, each believing he was under attack. Lances were lowered, shields were raised, a conflict ensued. Finally, one succeeded in unhorsing the other and, with a mighty thrust, drove his lance through the fallen man's heart. The victor dismounted, limped over to the motionless pile of armor, and lifted his adversary's mask. To his horror, the pale moonlight revealed the face of his own brother!

This story discloses the tragedy of all conflict: violence destroys the human family.

In an old Hasidic tale a rabbi asks his students, "How can we determine the hour of dawn, when the night ends and the day begins?"

One student suggests, "When, from a distance, you can distinguish between a dog and a sheep?"

"No," the rabbi answers.

Another student wonders, "Is it when you can distinguish between a fig tree and a grapevine?"

"No," the rabbi again answers.

"Please tell us, then," say the students.

"The hour of dawn" says the wise teacher, "is when you have enough light to look human beings in the face and recognize them as your brothers and sisters. Until then the darkness is still with us."

A Long, Dark Night

Any newspaper presents ample proof that morning has not yet dawned. South Africa, Central America, Afghanistan, Northern Ireland, Sudan, Cambodia, China—the names read like a litany of violence. And swords aren't exactly being beaten into plowshares in our own country: we spend 300 billion dollars a year arming ourselves to the eyeballs.

"In God we trust," our coins read, but don't believe it. "A 1986 Gallup poll revealed that for the first time the military establishment rather than the church was ranked as our most trusted institution." And our deepest faith commitments get passed on, one way or another, to our children. So sales of war toys have increased 700% since 1982, and 11 of the 20 best-selling toys have themes of violence, and the weekly television broadcast of war cartoons has increased from 1.5 hours in 1982 to 42 in 1987. Our children are learning well the real credo of American religion: in guns we trust.

Should we be surprised that through our city streets flow swelling cataracts of violent blood?

And the darkness doesn't seem any more dispersed by the light of family relationships. Studies indicate that domestic violence may be a problem in as many as sixty per cent of American homes. More than a million cases of child abuse are reported every year, and about two million wives are beaten each year by their husbands.

Conflicts in the world and in our homes are inevitable, I suppose, given the conflicts in our own hearts. To be sure, an inner light shines at times—when in quietness before God we feel loved and want nothing so much as to love in return, when the wind of an unusual circumstance blows back the curtain of the ordinary long enough for us to sense Mystery surrounding us and sustaining us, when young eyes, peering out of a face dedicated to dirt and mischief, look up at us with prodigal trust, when we feel almost bent over by the burden of blessings resting upon us—but even then, though the light shines, it shines against a hard, hostile darkness, flickering and stuttering its luminescence like an uncertain candle in a stubborn night. Yes, the large conflicts in the world outside us have smaller counterparts in the world inside us; too often the dogs of war have slipped their leashes to run wild through the irritations and tensions we allow to grow in the back yards of our private lives.

Confession time. In my desk drawer sits a concrete symbol, a sort of sacrament you could say, of my own hostility: a check from an insurance company made out to me for the sum of one cent. I had overpaid my last premium by this amount, and with upright integrity and generosity of spirit the accountants had wanted to keep their books properly balanced. So they sent me this paper penny . . . just after they canceled my policy. I had done the unforgivable:

I had actually needed my insurance and filed a claim—worse, *two* claims because our home had been burglarized on two different occasions. Well, that was stupid of me. Everyone knows that you only pay premiums to finance skyscrapers and to give yourself the illusion of protection from unscrupulous lawyers. Whatever possessed me?

I paid for my mistake; they dropped me faster than thieves falling from a ground-floor window. And now the check sits in my drawer. I know I should cash it (it's been two years). But then I think of a bookkeeper on the thirty-ninth floor of the building I helped fund, and I see exasperation contort his face as he tries to close my account, and I can sometimes hear him cuss as he debates whether to spend another quarter to send a reminder, and honestly, the pleasure is worth far more than the penny I could get by cashing the check.

I'm not proud of these feelings. But I report them in the interest of truth—the truth that the world's hostility, so easy to denounce with the righteous fury of a prophet, is *in essence* no different from my own hostility. As Isaiah confessed, "Woe is me! For I am a man of unclean lips, and I dwell in the midst of a people of unclean lips" (Is 6:5).

So when Jesus says, "Blessed are the peacemakers," I for one am not inclined to argue the point. I can easily imagine a blessedness coming with the laying down of arms in my own heart, not to mention the rest of the world.

The hero in Kurt Vonnegut's novel, *Slaughterhouse Five,* is an ex-prisoner of war who had witnessed one of history's most devastating fire bombings. He cannot endure the memory of the suffering caused by the massive air raid. So he fantasizes. He pictures the event as though seeing a movie running backward. Bombers full of holes and corpses and wounded men take off backward from their home base and fly, tail first, to the target area. As the planes hover over the rubble that was a city, bomb-bay doors open, and through a miraculous magnetism, raging fires shrink and bomb fragments lift out of the debris to ascend into fuselage bellies where they reassemble. Then they are flown, backward still, to their place of origin and dismantled. Finally, the people who had first made them bury the deadly components in the ground—in the author's words, "to hide them very cleverly so they would never hurt anybody again."

A wonderful dream, to see conflict reversed and debris cleaned up; to see where "the wolf shall dwell with the lamb, the leopard shall lie down with the kid" (Is 11:6); to catch a vision of the "holy mountain" of peace (11:9). "Blessed are the peacemakers"—indeed!

A Pause

But is peace always good? What about the peace of an unjust situation. Did Jesus imply we should *always* work to reduce conflict— regardless of the cost? For example, what does it mean to make peace in South Africa? Does it mean Blacks should stop protesting so Whites can continue to enjoy unfair advantages? Or—to use another example—what does it mean to make peace in an abusive marriage? Should a battered wife stifle her complaints and simply hope for the best?

This Beatitude would create no difficulty for us if Jesus had said, "Blessed are the peace *lovers* . . ." But peace*makers*—that's different. How do you make peace in tough situations like South Africa and abusive marriages? Should you even try? Don't some attempts to establish peaceable kingdoms result, finally, in reprehensible kingdoms?

Completing the Circle

The Bible, when it speaks of peace, refers to something not conveyed by the English word. In our language peace usually means the absence of conflict; it connotes something negative. But behind the seventh Beatitude stands the great Old Testament word *shalom*. This means much more than the absence of conflict; it connotes something positive. Perhaps the best way to translate it is *wholeness*. Biblical peace refers to a comprehensive well-being, a state of completeness. Dale Bruner describes it by using the image of a circle.

When the circle breaks, peacemakers try to complete it: they tie together severed relationships, they reconcile enemies, they heal wounds. Peacemaking isn't simply the abolition of warfare; it's the creation of welfare.

So shalom-makers in South Africa, to use our earlier example, will be justice-makers. That nation will never achieve peace, in the biblical sense, until justice flows like a river into every back alley of Soweto. The quieting of Black protests against the current state of affairs might indeed restore order and reduce conflict, but it would not create shalom.

And shalom-makers in abusive marriages will work for wholesome, mutually enriching relationships. The wife who makes peace in such a situation may actually need to intensify the problem by bringing it out of the closet of passive acquiescence into the light of honest acknowledgement; she may need to combat injustice by offering her husband the stark choice of counseling or divorce.

Peacemaking does far more than ease tensions in troublesome circumstances; it seeks healing, the wholeness intended by the Creator—even if this demands confrontation, a temporary commitment to discord in order to create a lasting harmony.

But how do we know which actions lead to shalom? Life is a

complicated business. Who has the foreknowledge and wisdom to choose with certainty the roads leading toward God's best? We need a guide. Who will show us the way?

Who else but the Prince of Peace?

Following the Prince

The preacher from Nazareth who blessed peacemakers is himself *the* peacemaking Son of God. We would do well to follow his example. Relying on our own sense of direction will get us lost in a wilderness of misplaced idealism; we will make matters worse, distancing ourselves and others from authentic peace.

If we stay with Jesus on the road he travelled toward shalom, we will soon discover that *we must be wholly dedicated to the will of God.*

One characteristic set Jesus apart from others, revealing his humility as the Son of God and his perfection as the Son of Man: his obedience. He never deviated from the road God chose for him. Sometimes it led him into verbal confrontation with the authorities ("Woe to you, scribes and Pharisees, hypocrites! For you are like whitewashed tombs . . ." Mt 23:27). At least once it led him into a physical confrontation as he tried to protect the poor from the moneychangers in the Temple. And yet by that same obedience he drank from a cup he wouldn't have chosen for himself; he accepted abuse, insults and lashings and spittle and thorns and nails and even death, without uttering a word in his own defense. Everything he did was in obedience to the King whose reign he announced and brought into the world. And for this reason he is the Prince of Peace.

How do you make peace? Begin by being obedient to God's will so far as you understand it.

Yes, in some situations God's will seems about as clear as a barrel of crude oil. More than once, when finding myself at a confusing crossroads, I've thought God could have been considerably more specific about whether I should turn right or left. And frankly, the Bible wasn't much help at those times—at least not as an unambiguous arbiter of my choices. That's because it isn't a book of rules covering every situation one might encounter in journeying from cradle to grave; it doesn't have an index in which one can look up, say, "money" and know for certain what to pay the gardener. No, the Bible is more like a symphony of witnesses whose music lifts us into the presence of Christ. We don't need a detailed road map, not really; we need a Guide who holds our hands when the fog thickens and who steadies us amidst the rocks and ruts and who strengthens us when weariness slows our steps.

Still, the Bible isn't without concrete help. As it takes us into the presence of Christ, Christ uses its witness to provide the *general* guidance we need. We know, for example, that all God's desires for us are summed up in two commandments: "You shall love the Lord your God with all your heart, and with all your soul, and with all your mind. This is the great and first commandment. And the second is like it, love your neighbor as yourself" (Mt 22:37-39). The rest of Scripture—through narratives and poems and parables and proverbs and epistles—refracts this light through various prisms to illumine segments of life, to illustrate how the law of love works itself out in different contexts.

When faced with a peacemaking task, then, we begin with self-examination. Are we being obedient? Are we acting out of love for God and love for our neighbors? We won't *always* be certain what to do, of course, but most of the time, in most circumstances, there won't be much doubt about the things that will lead to shalom. For the rest, we do our best and trust the grace of God.

Paying the Price

As we follow the Prince of Peace, the second thing we realize is that *we must be willing to bear the cost of shalom*. It can be expensive; it never goes on sale in the bargain basement. It can cost our pride, or a change of lifestyle, or even our lives. Some peacemakers in South Africa face jail and even death. Some women in abusive marriages throw away the "security" of a bad marriage to gain a good one. Peacemakers pay the price.

Don't most conflicts happen because we're trying to protect ourselves? We want to defend our social position, our reputation, our wealth. Feeling threatened, we do what we can to thrash opponents. Oh, we wouldn't use guns to blow them to the eternal judgment we think they deserve; certainly not. But we might wish for some selectively placed heart attacks. And we're not above nuking them with the more acceptable weapons of criticism and gossip and outmaneuvering. Anything to protect ourselves.

The people who will be most happy, the blessed ones, are those who pay the price of peace out of their own wallets. They absorb the conflict, as it were, by taking its pain unto themselves. They let go of self-protection in order to take hold of mutual shalom; they choose not to be above their Lord who gave himself up to the violence of this world to secure God's peace.

William Willimon tells the story of a student who, in his senior year of college, felt called by God to spread the gospel. But how? Should he go to seminary? Should he be a missionary?

Waiting for guidance, he took a job as a bus driver in Chicago. Driving his bus through the inner-city streets seemed an unlikely place for ministry. "Some place to serve Jesus," he thought to himself.

Every afternoon a group of young hoods boarded his bus for a ride downtown. They had a routine: they would get on, stroll past the fare box without putting a dime in, intimidate the other passengers and slouch to the back of the bus. They were daring him to make them pay.

Finally, the day came when he met them at the door and said, as courteously as he could, "Look guys, you've got to pay. Everybody else pays. It's not fair. If you don't pay, you can't ride." But instead of paying, they dragged him off the bus and beat him until he was unconscious, leaving him a bleeding, half-dead mess on the sidewalk.

The police caught the young assailants, easily identified by the terrified passengers on the bus and charged them with assault and battery.

At their trial a month later, the driver was called to testify against them. He was still bandaged from his beating, but hurting even more because he felt like a failure in his Christian faith; he hadn't convinced anyone about the truth of the gospel.

The defense lawyers pleaded for mercy, arguing that the boys were high-school seniors, and a conviction would keep them from graduating, marking their records for life. The judge was unmoved. As he prepared to sentence them, he turned to the driver to ask, "What would make you happy? What would make you feel better? You're the one who suffered from these worthless thugs."

"The thing which would make me happy," he said, "would be to serve their sentence for them, to go to jail on their behalf so that they could go back and finish school and do better."

The judge laughed in disbelief. "What? That's ridiculous! Absurd! Impractical! Nobody has ever done that!"

"Oh, yes He did," he said softly. "Oh yes, He did."

And this is why peacemakers shall be called children of God. Like their Lord, they pay the price, they suffer through to shalom.

High in the Andes Mountains stands a bronze statue of Christ, fashioned from old cannons. It marks the boundary between Argentina and Chile. Engraved in Spanish are these words: "Sooner shall these mountains crumble into dust than Argentines and Chileans break the peace sworn at the feet of Christ the Redeemer."

Blessed are those who create monuments of shalom at troublesome boundaries, for they shall be called children of God, brothers and sisters of the Prince of Peace.

Study Questions

1. What conflicts are going on in our world today?
2. What are some unresolved conflicts in your personal life?
3. What does it mean to be a peacemaker?
4. What role should the will of God play in our attempt to be peacemakers?
5. What does self-examination have to do with peacemaking?
6. What does the example of Christ teach you about peacemaking?
7. When we succeed in being peacemakers, what is our reward?

*B*lessed are those who are persecuted for righteousness' sake, for theirs is the kingdom of heaven. Blessed are you when men revile you and persecute you and utter all kinds of evil against you falsely on my account. Rejoice and be glad, for your reward is great in heaven, for so men persecuted the prophets who were before you.

9

AT ODDS
WITH THE WORLD

I wish I could summarize this book by promising that if the words of Jesus shape your life you will be successful. Unfortunately, I can't. Not if we mean by "success" a well-adjusted personality, an enviable niche in society, material comfort, and a fulfilled life. The Beatitudes do promise happiness, but that's something different. Happiness, if Jesus was right, has little in common with images of achievement featured in magazines like *People* and *Fortune;* it comes not from *having* but from *being.* It results, in other words, from a certain character.

Actually, having a character like the one Jesus described in the Beatitudes can put you at odds with the world. As though he anticipated this, Jesus concluded his description of kingdom people by saying, "Blessed are those who are persecuted for righteousness sake, for theirs is the kingdom of heaven" (Mt 5:10).

Against the Stream

Here's a Beatitude we hope never to need! We wouldn't dream of including persecution in our list of blessings. But it made it into Jesus' Top Eight, so we ought to try to understand why.

Let's begin by admitting that the idea of persecution jars our sensitivities. Besides the unpleasantness of the thing itself, we might be disappointed with a Christianity that doesn't deliver us from such a possibility. After all, we have enough trouble in life without getting more from our religion. The least it can do is help us cope with life, help us get along in the world.

And we do want to get along, don't we? We might smile condescendingly at adolescents who tear new jeans because every other kid in the school has the same size hole on the same leg on the same brand, but truth to tell, we conform just as readily to the characteristics of our peer group. The crowd exerts enormous pressure to "go with the flow."

Before running in my first ten-kilometer race, my physician advised me to take at least seven minutes for the first mile. I intended to do just that. But when the gun went off, hundreds of other runners surged forward, and my adrenalin surged too, and so also my competitive spirit, and at the one-mile marker I glanced at my watch and discovered only six minutes had passed. I wish I could report that I maintained the pace; unfortunately, by squandering my strength at the start I didn't have much left at the end. I should have run my *own* race.

But it's hard to run your own race. You don't need a Ph.D. in psychology to know that pressures to conform exert an almost ty-rannical influence on us from our earliest days. We may have trouble with arithmetic, but we have no difficulty learning that the teacher wants us to raise our hands before going to the bathroom and to refrain from throwing spit wads. We also discover, on the other hand, that our classmates couldn't care less about raised hands and love-launched spit wads. So we have a choice: whom do we please? We face this question again and again through childhood and ad-olescence and adulthood, and the way we answer it determines the kind of affirmation we receive. That affirmation then becomes an important block in the building of our personalities. In some ways who we *are*—at least, our self-understanding—is a consequence of how we have chosen to conform.

So if others run six-minute miles, well of course we'll break our backsides to keep pace with them, lest we're left behind and forced to swallow the lonely dust of nonconformity.

How then shall we understand the words of Jesus "Blessed are those who are persecuted . . ."? *Persecuted?* Why, it's hard enough being different, let alone being painfully rejected for it. This is one blessing we can do without!

But if we want to follow Christ and be numbered with his people, we have no other alternative. The Bible warns us to expect a heap of trouble from the rest of the world. "Indeed all who desire to live a godly life in Christ Jesus will be persecuted . . ." (2 Tim 3:12).

They will be persecuted, of course, because of their oddity. In a world of falsehood truth seems pretty strange. "You shall know the truth," Flannery O'Connor wrote, "and the truth shall make you odd." Or as T. S. Eliot put it in *The Family Reunion,* "In a world of fugitives the person taking the opposite direction will appear to run away." And breaking ranks is never popular; it can lead to social grief.

Being Odd for Christ's Sake

The early Christians certainly discovered the cost of being different, as many lost employment and social standing; some even lost their lives.

Clarence Jordan, founder of the interracial Koinonia Farm in Americus, Georgia, was once given a tour of a church. The pastor pointed with pride to the plush carpeting, padded pews and luxurious fixtures. As they stepped outside, he directed Jordan's attention to a huge cross atop the steeple. "The cross alone," he said, "cost us $10,000."

"You got cheated," Jordan told him. "Times were when Christians could get them for free."

And persecution is not a thing of the past. Today Christians in other countries expect persecution as a normal consequence of following Christ. Before the Berlin Wall came down I talked with young people in East Germany who, because they had chosen to be confirmed in the Church, knew they would find it difficult to attend a university and almost certainly would not be able to study the subjects of their choice. And there are believers in Nepal who defy their government's law against "proselytizing" by preaching the gospel and baptizing new converts, thus living with the constant threat of imprisonment. One Nepalese told my father, "If Christ died on the cross, what's five years in jail?" And more than a few Taiwanese and South Koreans and Central Americans, because of their commitment to Christ, have taken stands for social justice that have landed them in jail and sometimes even in the grave.

In the Lion's Den

Now, unless we think America has already become the kingdom of our Lord—a blasphemous notion by any reasonable assessment of the moral and spiritual health of our nation—we ought not to assume that we will escape the general experience of Christians through the ages. True enough, the difficulties of following Christ in this country may be less severe and far more subtle. We enjoy freedom of worship and a consequent plurality of religious beliefs that for the most part protect us from overt hostility. But that doesn't exempt us from being at odds with the world. In fact, the very subtlety of the opposition is itself a danger, for it desensitizes us to the differences between the kingdom of God and the kingdom of this world, and it creates the false expectation that life in these two realms can be harmonized in order to further our own security and prosperity.

We won't be thrown to lions, but we might be mauled by criticism from a society that doesn't enjoy having its selfishness exposed. We won't be locked in cells, but we might be imprisoned with no chance of promotion in a business world that worships the golden calf of upward mobility. We won't be sent to the gallows, but we might experience the slow death of ostracism from a group that doesn't want its ways of pleasure called into question. Jesus didn't promise his followers honorable recognition; he warned of hostile rejection.

But if we meet persecution—overt or subtle—we had better be sure it's for the right reason. Jesus didn't bless those on the prowl for persecution; he didn't congratulate self-righteous braggarts. Daniel might have been in the lion's den, but I doubt that he pulled any tails, and I don't think Jesus, in this Beatitude, was encouraging us to antagonize lions with pious bravado. No, what he said was, "Blessed are those who are persecuted *for righteousness' sake*." And in the commentary verse that follows, "Blessed are you when men revile you, and persecute you and utter all kinds of evil against you falsely *on my account."* If we find ourselves in trouble with the world, it had better be for the sake of righteousness, because of our commitment to Jesus Christ.

I can't list all possible ways to provoke opposition from the world, but given the subject of this book I must underscore how the Beatitudes conflict with the values of our surrounding culture. The poor in spirit are blessed by Jesus but not by people suckled at the breast of positive thinking. Those who mourn are blessed by Jesus but not by people running, without pausing for breath, from one entertainment to the next. The meek are blessed by Jesus but not by people brandishing weapons sharpened at assertiveness training seminars. Those who hunger and thirst for righteousness are blessed by Jesus but not people groping and grasping to fill an insatiable Black Hole of material desire. The merciful are blessed by Jesus but not by people too busy pursuing dreams of success to notice those on the bottom side of life. The pure in heart are blessed by Jesus but not by people intent on keeping all options open for new opportunities and experiences. The peacemakers are blessed by Jesus but not by people finding security in the accumulation of personal and national power. Those who decide to find happiness along the road mapped out by Jesus, in other words, will be traveling in a different direction from many around them. This may not automatically lead to persecution, but it might.

And then what? Rejoice! "Rejoice and be glad," Jesus said. The Greek phrase uses the verb which means "to leap exceedingly." When the lions growl, in other words, jump for joy.

Good News about Opposition

Rejoice, because *opposition clarifies one's true loyalties.* Our commitments remain theoretical until tested. But when we're forced to pay dearly for them, we show just how important they are to us.

Around A.D. 200 a man came to Tertullian, a theologian in Carthage, with a question still asked today. He wanted to know how he could be both a faithful Christian and successful in business. Tertullian let the man talk. The questioner knew he was supposed to be completely loyal to Christ, yet he wondered if compromises in principle and practice might be possible to improve his dealings with his pagan neighbors. Christianity at that time lacked a firm foothold in the Roman Empire; it was ridiculed by popular writers, scorned by proper Romans, and sporadically persecuted by the government. Tertullian's visitor felt socially battered and, what was worse, he feared his church membership would ruin him financially.

"What can I do; I must live!" cried the distraught man.

"Must you?" Tertullian replied.

Opposition can be the fire that refines, removing all that alloys and thereby weakens and cheapens our faith. A Cavalier soldier, before being killed in a battle against the Roundheads, had sold much of his property and given the money to the Royalist cause. His friends paid tribute to his memory by putting these words on his tombstone: "He served King Charles with a constant, dangerous, and expensive loyalty."

Blessed are those whose loyalties are clarified, and who serve the King of kings with unwavering courage, with extravagant fidelity.

Never Alone

And rejoice because in the midst of persecution *you will be in the best of company*. Friends and even family may fall away, but you won't be alone. Not only will you be walking a road beaten hard by the feet of prophets and martyrs, you will be accompanied by a Presence.

An Old Testament story illustrates what will happen. In the sixth century B.C. three young Hebrew exiles in Babylon—Shadrach, Meshach, and Abednego—disobeyed a royal edict by refusing to worship the golden image of King Nebuchadnezzar. When threatened with death in the burning, fiery furnace, they said, "Our God whom we serve is able to deliver us from the burning fiery furnace; and he will deliver us out of your hand, O king. But if not, be it known to you, O king, that we will not serve your gods or worship the golden image which you have set up" (Dan 3:17-18).

Then Nebuchadnezzar had the furnace heated seven times hotter than usual, and the three rebels were cast into the flames. But the king was astonished when he looked into the furnace. "I see four men loose," he said, "walking in the midst of the fire, and they are not hurt; and the appearance of the fourth is like a son of the gods" (3:25).

In the midst of a fiery ordeal, we will not be alone. The Son of God will be with us, the one who entered Jerusalem with a hero's welcome and within a week limped out of town with a cross on his back; the one persecuted for all righteousness' sake. Jesus was *the* rejected one—at odds with the religious establishment, at odds with the political powers, at odds with the world he came to save. But he will not be at odds with us, not when opposition assails; he knows what it's like to be in the fiery furnace, and he will stay with us, holding us to himself. "Who shall separate us from the love of Christ?" Paul asked the Christians in Rome. "Shall tribulation, or distress, or persecution, or famine, or nakedness, or peril, or sword? . . . No, in all these things we are more than conquerors through him who loved us" (Rom 8:35, 37).

One of the worst things that could happen to Christians during the days of the Roman persecution was to be sent to the mines of

New Midea in Africa. The prisoners were brutally whipped, marched through rocky valleys, burned by the sun, branded with hot irons, chained so they couldn't stand erect and sent into dark mines to work interminable hours. When those mines were opened some years ago, visitors discovered that the Christians had etched little words and slogans on the walls of the caves. Of all the words scratched in stone, two appear more than any others. One is the word *Christ;* the other, the word *life.*

Blessed are those who know the life-sustaining presence of Christ when the flames of persecution leap around them.

More Than Adequate Compensation

And finally, rejoice when you're at odds with the world because *you will receive a reward which will make it all worthwhile.* That's what Jesus promised in this Beatitude: "Blessed are those who are persecuted for righteousness sake, for theirs is the kingdom of heaven. Blessed are you when men revile you and persecute you. . . . Rejoice and be glad, for your reward is great in heaven" (Mt 5:10-12).

We don't speak much about heaven today. Perhaps we're nervous about being "so heavenly minded we're no earthly good"; perhaps we're uneasy about sounding old-fashioned with "pie in the sky" talk; perhaps we're embarrassed about using the reward motive to stimulate sacrificial devotion.

Whatever the reason, Scripture doesn't share our reticence. And that's encouraging, too, for we always get through hard times with the confidence that better times are coming. All-night study sessions are endured in hope of a degree; pressures at work are tolerated in hope of promotion; dry stretches in a marriage are lived through in hope of experiencing the joys of committed love; chemotherapy or radiation are suffered in hope of remission from cancer. We freely bear enormous difficulties if we think it will be worthwhile.

Delete the idea of heaven from our thinking and we will be reduced to a one-dimensional existence, "living," as Paul Minear phrased it, "without any invisible means of support."

When the Bible speaks of heaven, it uses poetically charged language—metaphors, similes, dramatic images—to describe a picture no eye has seen, music no ear has heard. So we shouldn't be distracted by details; we should, instead, let our hearts be sustained and our imaginations fired with an overall impression: things are going to be more than all right. The resurrection of Jesus from death is God's guarantee that grace will triumph over sin, good will triumph over evil and life will triumph over death. As for our present difficulties, "this slight momentary affliction," Paul said, "is achieving for us an eternal weight of glory beyond all comparison, because we look not to the things that are seen but to the things that are unseen" (2 Cor 4:17-18).

This unseen reality is not simply waiting for us in the future; it is present even now as the divine reign brought into our lives by Jesus Christ (the kingdom of God). Heaven will be the fulfillment of this, the completion of God's gracious work in us. Believing in it, hoping for it, has the effect of reviving our daily obedience and strengthening us for the long haul. We may have endured many trials on the journey, and we may have many more ahead of us, but we know we're not home yet.

Ray Stedman tells the story of an old missionary couple who had been working in Africa for many years and were returning to New York City to retire. With no pension and broken in health, they were discouraged, fearful of the future.

They happened to be booked on the same ship as Teddy Roosevelt, who was returning from a big-game hunting expedition. They watched the passengers trying to glimpse the great man, the crew fussing over him—all the fanfare accompanying the President's entourage.

But no one noticed them. The missionary said to his wife, "Something is wrong. Why should we have given our lives in faithful service for God in Africa all these many years and have no one care a thing about us? Here this man comes back from a hunting trip and everybody makes much over him, but nobody gives two hoots about us."

At the dock in New York a band was waiting to greet the President. The mayor and other dignitaries were present. Reporters were on hand to fill the papers with news of the event. But the missionary couple slipped off the ship unnoticed.

That night, in a cheap flat they found on the East Side, the man's spirit broke. He said to his wife, "I can't take this; God is not treating us fairly." His wife suggested he go in the bedroom and tell the Lord.

A short time later he came out of the bedroom with a face completely changed. His wife asked, "Dear, what happened?"

"The Lord settled it with me," he said. "I told him how bitter I was that the President should receive this tremendous homecoming, when no one met us as we returned home. And when I finished, it seemed as though the Lord put his hand on my shoulder and simply said, 'But you're not home yet!' "

Blessed are those who are at odds with the world; they are on their way home and great will be their reward.

Study Questions

1. What does the author mean when he says that happiness comes not from having but from being?
2. Can you recall times in your life when you chose conformity over persecution?
   How can persecution be a blessing?
3. Is it possible to seek our persecution for self-righteous reasons? Can you give an example?
4. How can persecution be a blessing?
5. How can our faith be strengthened when we are persecuted?
6. Who and what will we find when we are at odds with the world for Jesus' sake?
7. What is God's promise for those who are persecuted?
8. What does the kingdom of heaven mean to you?

Rejoice in
the Lord always;
Again I will say,
Rejoice!

CHAPTER

10

THE BUTTERFLY LANDS

What, then, is happiness? We've completed nine chapters of a book devoted to the subject, but still haven't defined it, at least directly. That wasn't an oversight. Had we begun with a definition, we would have had to use abstract categories drawn from philosophy or psychology, and most of us would have fallen asleep before the journey started. Well, and why not? In effect, we would have chosen our destination before leaving the garage. For certain tasks, of course, that's not a bad way to travel; when you need groceries or want to visit Grandma, it's a good idea to know where you're headed.

But learning is more an adventure in exploration: we set out in a general direction, but remain flexible in spirit, ready at any time to turn right or left depending on what we discover. We let the journey itself, in other words, determine the destination.

Our trip began with a question: How can we net this elusive butterfly called happiness? Along the way of discovery we stopped, as if pausing at different lookout points, at each Beatitude of Jesus. Jesus had some specific and often surprising things to say about happiness, and by staying with him, by looking where he looked and turning where he turned, we have come, I trust, to a place of deeper understanding where we can describe more accurately the flight pattern of this butterfly we would all like to catch.

By Way of Negation

Perhaps it's easiest to begin by summarizing what happiness is *not*. Happiness is not feeling satisfied with oneself; Jesus blessed the poor in spirit. Happiness is not feeling cheerful; Jesus blessed the mourners. Happiness is not feeling power over oneself and others; Jesus blessed the meek. Happiness is not feeling fulfilled; Jesus blessed those who hunger and thirst for righteousness. Happiness is not feeling detached from human suffering; Jesus blessed the merciful. Happiness is not feeling the freedom of many options; Jesus blessed the pure in heart. Happiness is not feeling delivered from stress and tension; Jesus blessed the peacemakers. Happiness is not feeling accepted by the world; Jesus blessed those who are persecuted.

If happiness isn't any of these feelings, it's safe to say it isn't connected with feelings at all. If it were, it would be subject to the most fickle part of the human personality. Feelings rise and fall like a roller coaster at the county fair. Many things (often uncontrollable) influence them: hormonal changes, a lover's compliment, a lover's complaint, the neighbor's dogs, the mood of the secretary, a pile of unpaid bills, good mail, bad mail, cloudy weather, and so on. A happiness dependent on feelings would be, at most, a fleeting, occasional experience.

A Solid Structure

It's best to think of happiness as an objective state which transcends emotional ups and downs.

Marriage offers a good analogy. Except for those dancing through the wine-and-roses days of a honeymoon, most married people would readily admit that the romantic feelings that got them into their present condition aren't as constant as the condition itself. A good marriage certainly enjoys seasons of passion, sheer delight in the other. But even the best marriages know other times, too, when the emotional atmosphere is as inviting as morning-mouth breath. The state of being married, in other words, transcends the many feelings connected with it. Marriage sets a protective framework around the relationship that makes possible the free rise and fall of feelings. Romantic feelings may lead into marriage, but ever after the marriage surrounds and supports those feelings, providing an ongoing stability that fickle emotions can never provide.

Happiness is a condition like marriage, an objective state of being that provides a foundation and structure in which all sorts of feelings dwell together, rather like members of a family who, though not always getting along, share life under the same roof. Though sometimes torn by tensions and weakened by problems, they're a good family; they have a wholeness that can only be described as joy.

With this image of happiness as a solid structure housing our feelings, we can see how someone, relying only on feelings as an indicator, may be happy but not know it, and conversely, how someone may think he or she is happy but really isn't.

Picture two scenes. The first, a strong stone house in which a family is squabbling; the teen-age son dented the new car, let's say, and the father is threatening to take it out of his allowance. The situation doesn't *feel* happy.

The second scene, a paper shack in which a family is at peace; there's much laughter, and things are as warm and wonderful as an old episode from Father Knows Best. The situation *feels* very happy.

But now imagine a hurricane bearing down on both houses. Where would you rather be? The family in the stone house, though obviously going through a hard time, will survive and experience good times yet to come; they are in a happy condition. But the family in the paper shack, though laughing, won't survive to hear another joke; they are in an unhappy condition.

Like a solid structure, happiness houses the various emotions we feel through life's ups and downs. It holds us together, as it were, making possible a life of wholeness.

The Shape of the Structure

Can we describe more accurately this framework of happiness? The Beatitudes show the beams and braces necessary to build a character that will house our various emotions within walls of long-term wholeness. We have examined them chapter by chapter. But now we should stand back and look at all eight as a whole. What can we say about them in general?

The most important thing is this: they portray human life that is conformed to the will of God. For this reason they point the way to happiness. God, as our Creator, knows us better than we know ourselves; God knows the *attitudes* that ought to *be* (be-attitudes) for us to grow into maturity, for us to build characters able to hold us together against the storms of life and the ravages of time. God knows, in other words, what will make us happy in the long run.

So when Jesus, God's Son, came into our world, he showed the way to this blessedness. The poor in spirit, the mourners, the meek, the hungry and thirsty for righteousness, the merciful, the pure in heart, the peacemakers, the persecuted—these people live in the center of God's will, and thus are on the way toward fulfilling their destiny as human beings.

I had just flown into Accra, the capital of Ghana. The sights and sounds and smells had hit me with great force, and I was still reeling from culture shock. Richie Kusterbeck had mercifully delivered me out of the chaos of the airport, taken me to a hotel room (where I began to wish there were no lights so I wouldn't have to see the spiders crawling across my bed), and led me to a deserted restaurant for dinner. We were seated over something resembling burgers and fries, but strange enough to make me wonder, when Richie started describing their first year as missionaries. He and his wife, Kae, had taken their one-year-old son to Donkorkrom Presbyterian Hospital (it takes six hours worth of bouncing bones in a Land Rover to get there from Accra), where he assumed responsibilities as Administrator and Chaplain. All three had had diarrhea for the first six months; Richie had had malaria twice. The stories he told of getting their belongings through the Ghanaian bureaucracy would be believed only by someone who has lived in West Africa. Richie wasn't complaining; not at all. He was simply explaining what things had been like—a period of great stress and loneliness.

I didn't know what to say. I simply shook my head and scraped what looked like dishwater-soaked lettuce off my burger. And then Richie said something I will never forget. He leaned way back in his chair, took his beer and lifted it as though he were offering a toast, and said with his no-nonsense, take-it-or-leave-it Brooklyn accent, "Hey! My favorite place to be is in the center of God's will!"

The best place for all of us, whether we realize it or not, is in the center of God's will. And God's will for all of us, whether in Donkorkrom or Detroit or Durango, is to *be* a certain kind of person. Jesus' Beatitudes show us the structure of life—the attitudes and lifestyle—that pleases God, that fulfills God's purposes for us.

And notice: those who please God are the blessed ones. By having characters constructed according to God's blueprints, they build houses of happiness for themselves. Yes, they continue to have "down" days of restlessness and frustration, as well as "up" days of peace and fulfillment, but all this happens within a framework of blessedness that keeps them together in wholeness and protects against the onslaught of storms, and promises to keep standing in the future.

Butterfly on the Shoulder

In the first chapter of this book, I likened the pursuit of happiness to trying to catch a butterfly that keeps slipping through the net of our grim determination. By now it should be clear that happiness is not something you capture; it has nothing to do with attainment. This is why efforts to seize it through material things or relationships or accomplishments always fail. Happiness isn't a matter of *having* but of *being*.

When we turn our attention to other things—to receiving God's grace in poverty of spirit, to grieving over human misery, to being gentle with ourselves and others, to hungering and thirsting for righteousness, to showing mercy, to focusing on God in singleness of heart, to making peace, to standing at odds with the world—and forget all about finding happiness, happiness comes. Call it a paradox if you wish or call it a gracious gift: when we give up the futile pursuit, the butterfly lands on our shoulders. Happiness comes not because we have attained anything but because we have become something—we have become people who live at the center of God's will.

The butterfly lands, actually, because God comes. A character has been constructed in which God feels at home. The result is called blessedness, a happiness far deeper and more enduring than any pleasure this world offers. God comes, and with God comes Love— passionate, aggressive, eternal. And with Love comes Joy, the Joy for which we have been striving and hoping against hope, the Joy for which we have been created.

Happiness is thus something of a mystery. The reason we can't define it precisely is because it partakes of transcendence. It comes with the presence of God, and that can never be held neatly within the confines of reason and language.

Brennan Manning, in his book *Lion and Lamb*, refers to *Gideon*, a play by Paddy Chayefsky, a Brooklyn Jew.

Gideon is out in the desert in his tent a thousand miles from nowhere, feeling deserted and rejected by God. One night, God breaks into the tent and Gideon is seduced, ravished, over-come, burnt by the wild fire of God's love. He is up all night, pacing back and forth in his tent. Finally dawn comes, and Gideon in his Brooklyn Jewish accent cries out, "God, Oh God, all night long I've thought of nuttin' but You, nuttin' but You. I'm caught up in the rapture of love. God, I want to take You into my tent, wrap you up, and keep You all to myself. God, hey, God tell me that You love me."

God answers, "I love you, Gideon."

"Yeh, tell me again, God."

"I love you, Gideon."

Gideon scratches his head. "I don't understand. Why? Why do you love?"

And God scratches *His* head and answers, "I really don't know. Sometimes, My Gideon, passion is unreasonable."

We may not fully understand the passion of God, but its ravishing presence can't be denied as it overpowers our self-centeredness and burns the coldness out of our hearts.

How can we be people in whom God feels at home? How can we build characters in which the blessed presence of God is pleased to dwell? How can we become the kind of people Jesus described in the Beatitudes? How can we change habits of mind and behavior that seem as inescapable as deep, never-ending ruts?

We must be careful here; we're walking on slippery ground. We may easily assume that the Beatitudes are like everything else we've seized to try to satisfy our hunger for happiness: something more to attain, a list of things to achieve. But happiness, as I've said, isn't a matter of having; it's a matter of being.

The Kingdom of Grace

The Beatitudes describe kingdom people, men and women whose lives have been transformed by the reign of God. The first characteristic of this reign is *grace*. Jesus not only announced the kingdom; he brought it as a gift.

We cannot force our way into God's realm; we cannot storm the gates with impeccable piety; we cannot hoist ourselves over the back wall with straining spirituality. Citizenship in this kingdom cannot be bought for any price—not even with the currency of good intentions.

But Jesus offers it to us, freely. He brought it into our midst through his life in the flesh. He walked among us as a man subject to all the frustrations and temptations and sufferings of human life, and yet he lived in perfect conformity to the will of God. This God-ward movement of his life wasn't simply a model for us to emulate; it was far more. He lived the kingdom life for us, as our representative.

So the Jesus who blessed the poor in spirit and the mourners and the meek and those hungry for righteousness and the merciful and the pure in heart and the peacemakers and the persecuted—this Jesus was himself *the* Blessed One. He fulfilled these Beatitudes in his own life.

What makes this good news for us is this: God has decided— for no reason other than an astonishing, incomprehensible, aggressively tender love—to judge our lives from the perspective of Jesus' life. When Jesus offered up his life in obedience to God, he did so as our representative, on our behalf. So completely did he identify with us that he took even our failures upon himself. He accepted responsibility for the condemnation we deserve for our self-centered, disobedient attempts to find happiness, and he hung on a cross outside the gates of Jerusalem because of it.

The Teacher, in other words, is our Savior. The One who showed the way to happiness has removed the barrier of guilt standing between us and God, so that we can live and move and have our being in the joyous freedom of grace.

Perhaps you've felt guilt in reading this book and put it down more than once to see what was on television to try to silence an inner voice of criticism. I know how you feel. I've lived with this book longer than you, and I have too often had the hammer of despair pound my spirit; I've thought, if *this* is the way to happiness I had better make my peace with unhappiness. But to both of us

I declare the gospel: God's grace in Jesus Christ is bigger than our sin. Through obedience to the Blessed One, the blessedness he declared can be ours. We are now free to get up from the mud of failure and follow him into a new life without the burden of remorse weighing us down. The kingdom of God revealed in Jesus Christ is the reign of grace.

Father Hugh Donlon, in Andrew Greeley's novel *Ascent into Hell*, dazzles the congregation with spellbinding oratory. "We must remember," he proclaims, "that we do not earn God's forgiveness by our sorrow or by our reparation. God's love is a given. It is always there waiting patiently for us. We need only to turn to Him to receive it. He is pleased with our efforts but even more pleased with us. That's why He made us. You cannot earn God's love because He gave it to you before you started to earn it."

But poor Father Donlon. He preaches the truth, but hasn't applied the truth to himself. He lives by a very different theology; the God of grim justice dominates his life. Eventually, though, shipwreck and heartbreak force him to turn his words toward himself, to accept the amazing fact of divine grace as good news for himself.

Let's not make the same mistake. Our quest for happiness must begin with humble acceptance of God's mercy. Only in that freedom can we become blessed ones. We're back, of course, to the first Beatitude. The poor in spirit know they can rely on nothing other than the grace of God.

The Kingdom of Power

When we entrust ourselves to the grace of God in Jesus Christ, a new life starts for us. The second characteristic of God's reign is *power*. When the King comes, things happen; when God resides in us, reconstruction begins.

By raising Jesus from death, God promised the defeat of sin and death, the victory of grace and life. Easter morning proves the power of God's good purposes for us. Nothing will ever come between us and this love—not self-centeredness, not unhappiness, not death. God has given a pledge, and all heaven and earth can't take it from us.

And the first movement in the symphony of victory can now be played out in our lives. God doesn't forgive and then forget us, leaving us to our own resources to get from here to heaven. No, God can manifest resurrection power in us—today. The name for this gracious, powerful presence is the Holy Spirit. This Spirit, which is God residing within us, transforms us by re-directing our wills and reshaping our characters.

How, then, do we build characters in which God joyfully dwells? Well, we don't. We trust the grace revealed in Jesus Christ, and we open ourselves to the Holy Spirit. God does the rest.

We become kingdom people through the reign of the King who refashions us into the sort of men and women Jesus declared blessed. The King alone has power enough to dislodge and discomfit our self-centeredness; the King alone can turn us from the pathetic pursuit of the butterfly of happiness; the King alone can make us blessed.

The story is told of a mother who, wishing to encourage her son's musical abilities, bought tickets for a performance by Ignace Paderewski, Poland's famous concert pianist and prime minister.

When the night arrived, they found their seats near the front of the auditorium. Soon the mother started speaking with a friend, and, without her knowing it, the boy slipped away.

At eight o'clock the house lights dimmed, the stage lights came on, the crowd quieted, and the curtain opened. Only then did they notice a little boy on the bench of the grand Steinway innocently plunking out "Twinkle, Twinkle, Little Star."

His mother gasped, but before she could retrieve him the master appeared on stage and quickly moved to the keyboard. "Don't quit—keep playing," he whispered to the boy. Leaning over him, Paderewski reached around with his left hand and filled in a bass part, and with his right he added a running obbligato. Together, master and novice held the crowd mesmerized.

As we play our little tunes, with unruly fingers and botched notes, the Master comes and, with loving arms around us, creates music we could never play on our own.

So when Paul told the Philippians to rejoice, he added the important words, "in the Lord" (Phil 4:4). All true rejoicing happens in the Lord, in the One who not only points the way to happiness but who supplies the strength to achieve it.

Study Questions

1. Having read this book, how would you describe happiness? (You may want to begin by describing what happiness is not.)

2. As a whole, how do the Beatitudes portray human life?

3. Why do the Beatitudes point the way to happiness?

4. Choose one Beatitude each that (1) challenges you, (2) frightens you, (3) comforts you, and tell why.

5. How do we build our character in a way that we will receive God's blessing?

6. Describe "kingdom people."

7. How do we find the way to happiness and the strength to achieve it?

Notes

Chapter 1. The Quest for the Elusive Butterfly

12   "Why am I . . ." Diogenes Allen, *The Traces of God in a Frequently Hostile World* (Cowley, 1981), pp. 8-9.

12   "Studies indicate that . . ." Martin E. P. Seligman, "Boomer Blues," *Psychology Today,* October 1988, p. 50.

13   "We're here to . . ." as quoted in "The Meaning of Life," *Life Magazine,* December 1988, p. 80.

14   "He lived at . . ." Ernest T. Campbell, *Locked in a Room with Open Doors* (Waco, Tex.: Word, 1974), p. 23.

14   "In 1973 American . . ." "To Verify . . . ," *Leadership,* Winter 1989, p. 81.

14   "Lou Harris tells . . ." as cited by Tom Sine, "God's Will—And a Little Creativity," *Christianity Today,* February 17, 1989, p. 24.

14   "Of those who . . ." Tom Sine, "God's Will—And a Little Creativity," *Christianity Today,* p. 24.

15   "*Psychology Today* conducted . . ." Carin Rubenstein, in *Psychology Today,* May 1981, p. 42.

15   "A recent study . . ." *National Association of College Stores Campus Market Report,* March 1988.

18   "I found myself . . ." Arthur Miller, *Timebends* (New York: Harper and Row, 1987), p. 370.

18 "On the day . . ." Alan Paton, *Instrument of Thy Peace* (Collins, Fount Paperbacks, 1977), p. 104.

18 "It's tough to . . ." *Bits and Pieces,* February 1989, p. 1.

19 "I learned what . . ." Dan Wakefield, *Returning—A Spiritual Journey* (New York: Doubleday, 1988), pp. 198-99.

19 "Tom Wolfe's novel . . ." Tom Wolfe, *The Bonfire of the Vanities* (New York: Farrar, Straus, Giroux, 1987).

20 "In April 1988 . . ." James D. Acree, "To Illustrate . . ." *Leadership,* Fall 1988, p. 44.

21 "Fear not that . . ." *Bits and Pieces,* November 1988, p. 10.

23 "In speaking this. . . ." I am indebted to the articles by Bertram and Hauck on "makarios," in Gerhard Kittel, ed., and Geoffrey W. Bromiley, trans., *Theological Dictionary of the New Testament,* vol. 4 (Grand Rapids: Eerdmans, 1967), pp. 362-70.

24 "To tell the . . ." Saul Bellow, Herzog (New York: The Viking Press, 1964), p. 169.

Chapter 2. Good News for Those in the Valley

29 "Are you content . . ." as quoted in Elliot Wright, *Holy Company—Christian Heroes and Heroines* (New York: Macmillan, 1980), p. 10.

30 "to creep under . . ." Elliot Wright, *Holy Company—Christian Heroes and Heroines,* p. 10.

31 "Dear God, my . . ." from an article in *Working Mother,* June 1987.

34 "The arrangement of . . ." Frederick Dale Bruner, *The Christbook—A Historical/ Theological Commentary* (Waco: Word Books, 1987), p. 135.

34 "After what has . . ." as quoted in *Christianity Today,* June 12, l987, p. 38.

35 "The gospel of . . ." Richard Fox, *Reinhold Niebuhr—A Biography* (New York: Pantheon Books, 1985), p. 89.

36 "It is worth . . ." John V. Taylor, *The Go Between God* (New York: Oxford University Press, 1979), p. 128.

36 "In Nikos Kazantzakis's . . ." Nikos Kazantzakis, *Christ Recrucified* (London: Faber and Faber, 1962), pp. 186-87.

37 "The sermon on . . ." Frederick Dale Bruner, *The Christbook—A Historical/ Theological Commentary,* p. 137.

Chapter 3: In Praise of Grief

44 "the number of . . ." as quoted in Robert Raines, *Creative Brooding* (New York: Macmillan, 1966), p. 11.

50   "We must begin . . ." Karl Barth, Church Dogmatics—IV/2, trans. G. W. Bromiley (Edinburgh: T. and T. Clark, 1958), p. 221.

Chapter 4. The Strength of Gentleness
59   "I want this . . ." as quoted in Sales Upbeat, Vol. C/No. 4.
60   "two hundred seventy . . ." Judith C. Lechman, The Spirituality of Gentleness—Growing Toward Wholeness (San Francisco: Harper and Row, 1987), pp. 2-3.
61   "So when she . . ." Henry Beard, Miss Piggy's Guide to Life (New York: Macmillan, 1981), pp. 3-4.
62   "After each surgery . . ." Lloyd Shearer, Parade, 1986.
63   "renounce every right . . ." Dietrich Bonhoeffer, The Cost of Discipleship, trans. R. H. Fuller (London: SCM Press, 1959), p. 99.
68   "Whenever Hollywood cranks . . ." Frederick Buechner, Peculiar Treasures—A Biblical Who's Who (San Francisco: Harper and Row, 1979), p. 111.
69   "the poise of . . ." F. Dale Bruner, The Christbook (Waco: Word Books, 1987), p. 141.
70   "when the kingdom . . ." Dietrich Bonhoeffer, The Cost of Discipleship, pp. 99-100.

Chapter 5. The Blessed Longing
79   "Usually the verbs . . ." William Barclay, The Gospel According to Matthew—Vol. I (Philadelphia: Westminster, 1956), p. 96.
80   "There is an . . ." Diogenes Allen, Traces of God in a Frequently Hostile World (Cowley, 1981), pp. 100-101.
80   "Do you want . . ." as quoted by Alton H. McEachern, "Sermon Series on the Beatitudes Continues," Preaching, May/June 1987, p. 36.
85   "Every time you . . ." C. S. Lewis, Mere Christianity (New York: Macmillan, 1960), pp. 86-87.

Chapter 6. The Gift of Mercy
93   "Jacinta Diaz was . . ." Peter Morgan, Story Weaving (St. Louis: CBP Press, 1986), pp. 18-19.
95   "In January 1988 . . ." Time, Feb. 22, 1988, p. 31.
97   "Calvin Coolidge, during . . ." Clifton Fadiman, The Little, Brown Book of Anecdotes (Boston: Little, Brown, 1985), p. 140.
100   "Following World War . . ." Paul Brand and Philip Yancey, Fearfully and Wonderfully Made (Grand Rapids: Zondervan, 1980), p. 206.

101 "Louis B. Mayer . . ." *Bits and Pieces,* November 1987, pp. 3-4.

103 "She was sitting . . ." Paul Brand and Philip Yancey, *In His Image* (Grand Rapids: Zondervan, 1984), pp. 43-46.

Chapter 7. Clear at the Center

109 "the place to . . ." as quoted in Keith Albow, "The Fault Isn't Heart's—It's Ours," *U.S. News and World Report,* Jan. 25, 1988, p. 9.

109 "The modern use . . ." Frederick Dale Bruner, *The Christbook—A Historical/ Theological Commentary* (Waco: Word Books, 1987), p. 147.

112 "A columnist for . . .' " Barry Lorge, *The San Diego Union,* April 24, 1987.

112 "David Seamands tells . . ." David Seamands, "Private Sins of Public Ministry," *Leadership,* Winter 1988, p. 27.

114 "The pure in . . ." Dietrich Bonhoeffer, *The Cost of* Discipleship, trans. R. H. Fuller (London: SCM Press, 1959), p. 101.

Chapter 8. Waging Peace

125 "One night during . . ." John Claypool, *Opening Blind Eyes* (Nashville: Abingdon, 1983), p. 103.

126 "In an old . . ." as told by Henri Nouwen, "Adam's Peace," *World Vision,* August-September, 1988, p. 7.

126 " 'A 1986 Gallup . . .' " Donald G. Bloesch, "No Other Gospel," *Presbyterian Communique,* January/February 1988, p. 8.

126 "So sales of . . ." *International Christian Digest,* May 1987, p. 48.

130 "Dale Bruner describes . . ." F. Dale Bruner, *The Christbook—A Historical/ Theological Commentary* (Waco: Word, 1987), p. 149.

133 "William Willimon tells . . ." William Willimon, *Preaching,* March/April 1988, p. 25.

Chapter 9. At Odds with the World

143 "You shall know . . ." as quoted by Leonard I. Sweet, "From Catacomb to Basilica: The Dilemma Oldline Protestantism," *The Christian Century,* Nov. 2, 1988, p. 982.

143 "In a world . . ." Leonard I. Sweet, *The Christian Century,* pp. 982.

144 "Clarence Jordan, founder . . ." as quoted in *Preaching,* July/August 1988, p. 34.

147 "Around A.D. 200 . . ." Wright, *Holy Company,* p. 225.

147 "A Cavalier soldier . . ." as quoted by James Cox, *The Minister's Manual for 1988* (San Francisco: Harper and Row, 1987), p. 313.

150   " 'living,' as Paul . . ." as quoted in Eugene Peterson, *Reversed Thunder* (San Francisco: Harper and Row, 1988), p. 168.

150   "Ray Stedman tells . . ." Ray Stedman, *Talking to My Father,* as condensed in *Leadership,* Summer 1987, p. 48.

Chapter 10. The Butterfly Lands

163   "Gideon is out . . ." Brennan Manning, *Lion and Lamb* (Old Tappan: Chosen, 1986), pp. 96-97.

167   "The story is . . ." as told by Darrel L. Anderson, *Leadership,* Spring 1983, p. 92.